MW00683268

# ABOUT THE AUTHOR

**Max Carbone** is a team strategic planning expert who is a student and player of the great games of golf, business and life.

Max is a highly sought after leadership advisor, author, facilitator, strategist, executive coach and an entertaining speaker who has worked with hundreds of leaders and teams to develop and execute successful winning business and personal strategic game plans.

Through an in-depth application of leadership practices, business strategy, marketing, psychology, the subconscious mind, organizational development, personal development and peak performance, Max helps leaders drive results in the games of golf, business and life.

Through his consulting practice, Team Works Management, Max has assisted blue-chip companies, leading high growth technology enterprises, entrepreneurial ventures, family owned companies, venture capital backed companies, corporate organizations, legal & accounting partnerships, numerous golf and resort businesses, various business associations, government organizations, not-for-profits and charitable organizations. Strategic expertise has been provided to startups, turnarounds, corporate mergers, leadership team dispute resolution, rightsizing, marketing research, new strategy implementation, re-organizations and building high growth teams.

Clients have included companies and brands like Alliance Atlantis, AT&T, Chubb Security, Coca-Cola, Molsons, Powerade, Corona, TD Bank, Royal LePage, CB Richard Ellis, Chubb Security, MuchMusic, Canadian Venture Capital Association, Association for Corporate Growth, Young President's Organization and many, many more.

Max has been involved in hundreds of real situations to help leaders and teams create a positive new vision for their future, resolve their personal and team challenges so that they can realize their personal, career and sometimes even their elusive golfing goals!

- MBA - Schulich School of Business- A leading North American business school

- BA - University of Western Ontario – Psychology & Administrative Studies

- US & Canadian Golf Teachers Federation Member

- 2000 North American Golf Teachers Federation Champion

- Ontario Hypnosis Institute –Hypnosis & Neuro Linguistics Programming Certification

- Thomas International - Behavioral Assessment Certification

- HRPAO - Member

- Ontario Environment Industry Association – Member

- Association for Corporate Growth - Member

Max is married to Anna Carbone and together they raise their three teenaged daughters, Julia, Marla and Tara. He is the proud son of Dr. Renzo Carbone an award-winning author and internationally recognized physician whose career focused on helping people lead better lives through medicine, psychology, health and wellness communication.

In *Scoring Eagles!* Max shares the proven success strategies elite players in the games of golf, business and life consistently apply to help them realize their potential and drive results in the games they love!

# Scoring Eagles!

Play Your Best!

Max

LIFESUCCESS PUBLISHING, LLC
8900 E Pinnacle Peak Road, Suite D240
Scottsdale, AZ 85255

Telephone:    800.473.7134
Fax:          480.661.1014
E-mail:       admin@lifesuccesspublishing.com
ISBN:         978-1-59930-045-0
Cover :       Lloyd Arbour & LifeSuccess Publishing
Layout:       Lloyd Arbour & LifeSuccess Publishing

COMPANIES, ORGANIZATIONS, INSTITUTIONS, AND
INDUSTRY PUBLICATIONS:  Quantity discounts are available on bulk
purchases of this book for reselling, educational purposes, subscription
incentives, gifts, sponsorship, or fundraising.  Special books or book
excerpts can also be created to fit specific needs such as private labeling
with your logo on the cover and a message from a VIP printed inside.
For more information please contact our Special Sales Department at
LifeSuccess Publishing.

Printed in Canada

# SCORING EAGLES!

## *DRIVING RESULTS*
### *IN GOLF, BUSINESS AND LIFE*

**Max Carbone,** MBA

# DEDICATION

To Mom & Dad who showed
us how to lead a good life,

To Julia, Marla & Tara whose
future looks so bright,

& To Anna who patiently
helps us realize our potential.

# ACKNOWLEDGEMENTS

For more than twenty-five years I have had the opportunity to work in various capacities with numerous leaders and teams from a wide variety of organizations and cultures.

My journey and experiences through several industries and organizations in various stages of their development have afforded me the opportunity to experience working with dynamic entrepreneurs, powerful corporate executives, expert marketers, creative geniuses, driven sales professionals, turnaround artists, golfing champions, personal development gurus, association leaders, charity crusaders, principled board members, not-for-profit drivers, passionate NGOs and yes, even great government and political leaders. Their collective insights, experiences, energy, work, talent and passion have been instrumental in helping me glimpse some of the common traits, behaviors and practices that enable great leaders and their teams to positively drive results.

Any valuable lessons that you find within the pages that follow have been made possible thanks to the input and experiences gleaned from helping those leaders, educators, mentors and team members.

Although there are far too many people to mention by name, I sincerely wish to acknowledge and thank all of those people whose spirit I have been fortunate enough to encounter and who have shared their tremendous insights & experiences. May their knowledge help you in your ongoing quest to improve your game!

# TABLE OF CONTENTS

CHAPTER 1: The Frost Delay ............................................. 15

CHAPTER 2: The Outward Nine ...................................... 21

CHAPTER 3: The Turning Point ...................................... 33

CHAPTER 4: The Inward Nine ........................................ 39

CHAPTER 5: How Leaders Drive Results ....................... 59

CHAPTER 6: The Spring Ahead ...................................... 91

CHAPTER 7: Eagles & Teams .......................................... 95

# CHAPTER 1
## THE FROST DELAY

# CHAPTER 1

It was a remarkable autumn day, one of the last great sunny days to play golf before the long darkness of winter. The morning sky was incredibly blue as the low-lying sun magnified the intensity of both the color of the sky and the late fall green grass. The air was crisp as the leaves barely held on to their branches for the last spectacular display of autumn colors. The previous night's chill left a blanket of sparkling frost on the course. Due to the long frost delay, the last of the few avid late season players decided to forgo the round, leaving the course wide open.

Jake Barrett sauntered from the putting green where he had been half-heartedly practicing his short game and headed towards the clubhouse. As he walked, he reflected on the fact that his golf game seemed equally as bad as the last quarter's results at work. His recent arguing with his spouse and two young children at home weren't helping matters much, either. And now as if to add insult to injury, his usual golfing group abandoned him, and he had to wait for the frost to lift before he could play his last golf round of the season. Alone, Jake decided to hang out at the club since he didn't feel like going to the office to do paperwork and wasn't in the mood to head home. A natural born winner, Jake sat inside the virtually empty clubhouse feeling like he just couldn't break his ongoing streak of bad karma.

Finally, after a frost delay of almost three hours, Jake heard the announcement that the greens keeper had finally cleared the course for play. Jake spoke briefly with the starter, who let him know that the first tee was now available for him to tee off any time he liked. As Jake made his way to the first tee, he spotted Ken Burns making his way to the starters' cabin. Jake and Ken were casual acquaintances. They knew of one another from their business activities that occasionally brought them into contact with one another but had never played golf together. Their love of the game outweighed the disadvantage of playing in cooler weather.

Ken was quite a few years older than Jake and nearing the end of his business career. He had been a real pioneer in the recycling industries and was highly respected by people in his field. Ken had been an extremely successful leader and known for his ability to inspire others. He was positive, dynamic and visionary. His success stemmed from his passion for his customers, his consideration for his employees and his concern for the environment. Jake was looking forward to playing golf with such a renowned leader.

Ken was born into relatively modest beginnings and grew to be a real leader in his game. He pioneered the development of numerous recycling technologies and was prolific in developing both his company and the industry. He was even instrumental in helping to build great competitors! Most importantly, Ken developed his people, built winning teams, and attracted hordes of new customers. He was able to recruit and inspire a passionate army of followers, who both learned from and emulated his behavior. These followers performed exceptional actions on their team's behalf. Being a gifted leader, Ken had an intuitive knowledge of how to inspire people to follow his lead. Ken led the way with heart, passion, focus and determination. Although ambitious, Ken focused his ambition to envelop his entire team and make them all a great success.

Ken had recently arranged for a successor to takeover the reins of the company he once led, as now he wanted to spend more of his time with his family. His involvement consisted of being a board member and a strategic advisor to various ventures. Although Jake could see that Ken didn't have the spring in his step that younger men possessed, there still seemed to be a positive aura emanating from him. Ken had a great run in his day. He built a solid reputation, helped numerous other players succeed in their game, and was recognized as a great builder at all levels.

Jake was a generation younger then Ken and had yet to really hit his career stride. Jake possessed tremendous potential and talent. He was intelligent, driven and possessed the presence that great leaders seem to be able to generate. Jake was also an intense competitor. He was focused, analytical and a force to be reckoned with. His substantial capabilities and determination to succeed put him head and shoulders above the average person.

Recently, Jake was recruited to be the leader of an entrepreneurial public venture in the clean technology field. Jake's company was developing, manufacturing and marketing a variety of clean-technology alternative energy products and services that reduced $CO_2$ emissions. The company's technology and team was still in the incipient stages of development, but many investors thought the venture had great potential. There was certainly a great need for their offerings, but the team just couldn't get the momentum required to achieve a quantum leap improvement in the company's technology, to reduce their pricing, to grow the markets and to drive real business results. Jake was a determined man and really wanted to make his company successful, not only because of his substantial equity holdings and options in the firm, but also because he realized how necessary these new technologies would be to improving the health of the planet for future generations. However, his frustration continually mounted as he realized he wasn't getting anywhere close to realizing the venture's true potential.

Although Jake possessed tremendous talent and abilities, he seemed unable to inspire the passion, commitment, and loyalty from his people that Ken had been able to generate during his career. Jake had all the talent to be a tremendous player and competitor, but was not yet able to realize his leadership potential. Jake was becoming frustrated, angry and distraught by the lack of results. He knew he was a talented player with exceptional capabilities, but wondered why he was unable to unlock the tremendous potential that lay within him.

Jake contemplated his dilemma while waiting to tee off. He thought about how he could quickly become a great leader who truly produced great successes and achievements. Though hungry to drive positive change, he was impatient with his lack of results. Recently, Jake had even considered giving up and finding another line of work in a less challenging arena. Jake knew that he had to reach out to get some advice, but didn't know where or maybe even how to look for leadership help.

On this fateful morning, the starter asked Jake if he would like to play a round with Ken. Jake slowly turned to introduce himself to Ken, who looked at him with a kind, almost fatherly smile. This was going to be the start of a spectacular game that Jake would never forget.

# CHAPTER 2
## THE OUTWARD NINE

# CHAPTER 2

Ken and Jake introduced themselves to one another. Ken enjoyed connecting with new people and was glad to have the opportunity to play with Jake today. Although they worked in different industries, they knew about one another, as both of their companies were in the clean technology game.

On the golf front, both players quickly learned they each carried a pretty respectable handicap of twelve, especially given the limited amount of time they were able to dedicate to playing the game. Jake was younger and stronger than Ken. He was a natural athlete with a solid swing and great mechanics. Jake had all the makings of a great power player. Although Ken was less able physically than he was in his younger years, he still could make the most of his abilities and play a pretty solid game.

With the cooler weather and the potential to lose balls in the autumn leaves, the players decided to play a straight-up match play competition rather than a more traditional stroke play game. The two men agreed to an eighteen-hole match and decided that the loser would treat the winner to a fine luncheon at the clubhouse. Ken won the "tee-toss" to see who went first.

While walking up to the tee, Ken quietly reflected on what a great gift it was to be alive and to be playing the great game on such a spectacular fall day. He loved being outdoors, and the game of golf had always helped to keep him grounded as it maintained his connection to the beauty of nature. Golf had been a great friend and perhaps even a great teacher to Ken. Thanks to the game, he had established many long-term relationships with friends, family, employees and customers. It was a great activity that he had been able to enjoy for his entire lifetime.

Golf was also a kind of a spiritual retreat for Ken. He learned great insights from playing the game about himself, about others and about the game of life. He applied these insights to improve his results in business and life. Indeed, golf served a multitude of purposes. Whenever he became frustrated at work or home, rather than taking it out on those around him, Ken would find a way to get to the range for a break. After taking a few swings at the ball, his negative emotions would lift, and he would return to being his calm, positive, centered self.

Ken also learned a tremendous amount about his team, suppliers and customers by how they played the game. When an individual played golf, regardless of their playing ability, Ken was able to read a great deal into their behavior and how they responded to the various situations that the game inevitably produced. Specifically, Ken could see that a person's personal behavior was reflected in their swing, their approach to the game and their attitude on the course. He observed that the vast majority of players tried their best to play such a challenging game. Most players abided by the rules, enjoyed the round, and tried to make the most of their abilities.

Over the years, he had come to recognize that extremes in behavior demonstrated on the golf course were a reflection of the same extremes in behavior that an individual would manifest in their business and personal lives. The majority of the players are positive, kind and optimistic. They do their best to play an extremely challenging game and give positive kudos and compliments to their fellow players. Sometimes, though, many players demonstrate the negative aspects of their personality when things don't go as planned. All sorts of aspects of people's personalities emerged, they became: controlling, indifferent, timid, serious, ultra-competitive and/or arrogant.

If the game being played was purely a social activity or if the players were just learning the game, then Ken was the first one to offer a mulligan or two and would help others out with an occasional foot wedge so that they wouldn't get overly frustrated or embarrassed.

However, if avid players were playing the game in a competitive event or if the match was for money, Ken insisted that the players strictly adhered to the rules, values and spirit of the game. On a few occasions, he came across overly competitive individuals who, with a blatant lack of regard for the values of the game, tried to cheat their way to a win. Ken avoided all future relationships with such players, as he knew that their behavior in the game would be emulated in the games of business and life.

Ken knew that everyone had the potential to be a better person, and he himself was no exception. Because of this, he was constantly interested in improving himself and his abilities. Perhaps that's why the game of golf appealed to Ken. Golf is a complex, challenging game that anyone can play but that no one ever really masters. Throughout one's life, the game continually offers challenges and tremendous potential for ongoing improvement at the spiritual, mental and physical levels.

Well, now it was time to begin his round. No matter how many times Ken played the opening hole, he always took a fresh look down the fairway and admired it as if he had never played it before. This particular hole was a 460-yard par four dogleg left. It had a classic tree-lined fairway, and in the distance one could see that a large bunker protected the green. Ken reminded himself that the place to miss his drive was on the right side as it was much less penal than a miss on the left.

Tossing some grass into the air, Ken determined the direction of the breeze then looked up at the treetops to confirm it was flowing from the north. Having just come from the driving range, he felt comfortable with his swing. Ken enjoyed trying to work the ball both ways, but like the majority of players, he was generally more consistent playing a modest fade.

Ken planted his tee ball into the far right hand side of the tee blocks to open up the fairway for the left to right fade he intended to play. He stood behind the golf ball, envisioning a smooth swing that produced an imaginary ball flight starting down the left center of the fairway. He visualized a modest fade, and with the help of the gentle breeze, imagined the ball drifting back to the right half of the short grass. With a long deep breath, he closed his eyes for a moment, allowing his mind and body to almost let go of control as he moved into what seemed like a hypnotic trance some experts have called the zone.

Then Ken addressed the ball and with a determined but seemingly effortless swing, his driver powered the ball through the atmosphere. It soared toward the intimidating trees on the left, but quickly took the fade and rode the wind back to the right side. The ball landed in the right centre of the fairway and stopped short of the rough on the right side just inside the 150-yard marker. It was exactly the shot he had envisioned. His calm, confident attitude was clearly evident in his golf game. Ken smiled positively and offered the tee blocks up to Jake for his opening salvo.

Jake stomped his way up onto the mound where the first tee was situated. He played the game with power and aggression. Knowing that he had the ability to out-muscle Ken, Jake took a mighty practice swing. He loved to hit impressive drives and titanic iron shots. He could drive the ball a long way and loved the intimidation factor of the power game. Jake knew if he spanked the ball just right with his physical strength, using his titanium technology and having the advantage of a downhill hole, he could easily cut the corner and get the ball to around the 100-yard mark.

It was risky, but this was competition, and Jake loved to crush those he competed against.

Jake took command of the tee stabbing his ball and tee into the ground. Taking a couple more powerful practice swings, he committed himself to blasting a straight shot over the trees, cutting the corner of the dogleg to give him an easy, short pitch into the large receptive green. He grit his teeth, tightened up and then took a huge rip at the ball. Jack made solid contact, and the ball started directly down the aggressive line he had intended. Unbeknownst to Jake, he had come over the top of the ball with his extra effort and had imparted just a hair of a hook-spin onto it. The ball initially cruised easily over the trees at the corner of the dogleg and looked like a great shot. Then, as the ball's forward momentum started to decrease, the counter-clockwise spin began taking a greater effect and the ball veered left toward the denser grouping of trees ahead.

Ken closely followed Jake's shot then shuddered as he felt the ball rattle around in the thicker grouping of trees on the left side. He never liked to see a player's initial tee shot head into trouble. In anger, Jake cursed as he chopped his driver head down like an axe and drilled his tee deep enough into the planet to strike oil.

 The twosome walked quietly down the fairway together and came to Ken's ball first. From his lie on the fairway, Ken had a clear shot to the green. He once again went through his pre-shot routine and smoothed a modest five iron well over the hazardous bunker onto the back of the green where the ball rolled about forty feet past the pin. It was an unspectacular, but very safe shot.

Then, both players ventured into the woods on the left to locate Jake's ball. After searching for a few moments, they found his ball lodged between the roots of a tree. Jake's only shot was to punch the ball out backwards into the fairway. Jake, having no other option, took an eight iron and angrily chopped the ball back into the fairway roughly 140 yards away from the flagstick. He hated having to give up yardage, but had no other choice. Huffing back to his ball, Jake bladed a nine iron onto the back of the green where he was still farther away than Ken. Jake then tried to drive his putt for par into the cup but blew it twenty feet past the hole. Ken quietly studied his playing partner's actions curiously. After Jake finished putting, Ken gently stroked his approach putt to about two feet below the cup where Jake conceded the par to Ken and awarded him the first hole in their match.

As they walked to the second hole, Ken could sense Jake's anger and felt the tension mount. Ken wanted to have an enjoyable round with Jake, so he made a couple of positive comments about the weather and what a great final day of the season it was turning out to be. Ken asked Jake about how his business activities were doing. He heard that Jake was the leader of some exciting new clean technologies, but he was unaware that his firm was in some rough waters. Unfortunately, reminding Jake of the challenges at his work didn't help his focus or concentration on his golf game.

The second hole was a 400-yard uphill par four with the wind, once again blowing from left to right. The fairway was wide open and pretty flat up until the fairway bunker that jutted out from the right side into the fairway running about 260 to 300 yards away from the tee. The left side of the fairway was filled with heavy, thick rough and had a few majestic old trees in the far left. The green had one bunker on the right front of the green with the pin neatly tucked in behind the greenside bunker.

Ken took out his three-wood and played a flowing, carefree draw down the heart of the fairway. His ball came to rest well short of the fairway bunker. This left an uphill shot of 170 yards to a protected pin. Jake pulled out his driver hoping to blast his ball just left of the bunker onto the narrow ribbon of fairway next to it.

He smoked his drive all right, but pushed it a hair right. Although the ball didn't find its way into the bunker, he did miss the fairway and ended up a yard or two into the deep, damp rough next to the bunker with only another 120 uphill yards remaining to play.

Ken was away first and took out his five iron once again, plenty of club to avoid the treacherous greenside bunker that was short and right. He aimed well to the far left side of the green to avoid the nasty, ball-collecting burial ground of sand. At the last critical moment of his swing, trying to give it a little extra, Ken came out of his swing and pulled his shot left of his intended target. Fortunately, his natural fade and the wind brought the ball back to within a few yards of the left side of the green. Ken was left with a relatively easy 60-foot chip to the hole.

Jake, meanwhile, had 120 uphill yards from a deep buried lie in the cool, wet rough. He decided to hit this shot way up high, directly over the steep-faced greenside bunker ahead, hoping it would stop on the down slope of the green and end up somewhere near the pin. He took out his pitching wedge to do the job. Jake knew he had to get the shot up really high in order to stop it for a reasonable birdie putt. Jake made a great swing, but the heavy grass bit into his clubface just enough to de-loft the club a couple of degrees and caused the ball to have a lower trajectory than planned. The shot looked great in the air, but it ended up a yard short of perfect. Unfortunately, Jake's ball hit the face of the greenside bunker and dribbled down into the abyss of sand below. Jake fumed. He had manufactured two shots that were both a hair away from excellence. Now he faced a brutal bunker shot. He couldn't believe his ongoing bad streak of luck.

Ken walked up towards the fringe and took out his eight-iron. Using a putting-type stroke, he sent his modest shot about twelve feet short of the hole to leave him with a reasonable uphill par attempt. Then he waited patiently for Jake to attempt his exit from the bunker.

Jake climbed down into the sand-filled pit. He knew he had to hit this shot perfectly in order to get it high enough to clear the bunker and then land soft enough to stop somewhere near the pin. Jake took a wide stance and an even wider, shallow swing at the sand behind the ball. He produced a spectacular sand shot that went unbelievably high. The ball easily cleared the lip of the bunker and had all the makings of a tour quality shot. It landed softly on the thick grass just beyond the edge of the bunker, but rather than trickling out onto the green like Jake had hoped, it was grabbed by the rough and just seemed to stick there, a foot short of reaching the green.

Jake leapt out of the bunker to see what kind of shot he was left with, and once again, he couldn't believe his misfortune. He had just made an incredible bunker shot that was virtually perfect and now faced a slippery downhill shot out of another gnarly lie in the rough.

Jake took a look at his lie and noticed it was really sitting down deep in the long, damp grass. He could either try a punch shot to get it running, but that would likely leave him a longish putt, or he could try to hit a fancy shot with his lob wedge to pop it up and stop it close to the cup. Jake chose the latter. He took a couple of good practice swings then stepped up to hit the ball.

Jake swung through the shot and the thick grass once again firmly grabbed his club. He twitched involuntarily and then forced his club through the grass, which caused him to double hit the ball and knocked it thirty feet past the cup. He grimaced and had an almost uncontrollable desire to snap the shaft of his wedge across his knee, but somehow resisted the temptation. With his double hit, Jake was now laying five and was hot as Hades. He grabbed his putter and without reading the putt, he slammed the ball directly into the back of the hole at warp speed for a painful double bogey six.

Meanwhile, Ken effortlessly nursed his twelve-foot par putt to a foot below the cup and proceeded to tap it in for bogey five and quickly went two up in their match.

The men walked silently over to the nearby third hole, a picturesque 180-yard par three over a menacing pond to a large, well bunkered and contoured green. Today's pin was cut directly in the center of the green. The tee shot was head on into the wind that had picked up somewhat since they started playing their round. Ken was up first once again.

Now Ken knew he could get there on a normal day with a four or five iron. Given the wind and the cooler conditions, he decided to use his nineteen-degree utility club to ensure he would clear the water. Ken went through his pre-shot routine and once again aimed to the left part of the green and played a fade hoping to land somewhere on the green. He hit a good shot, but over cut it a bit. The wind enhanced the spin's effect and pushed the ball into the bunker on the right of the green.

Meanwhile, Jake was still steamed from his overdose of bad fortune on the previous hole. He pulled out a six iron, the club he would normally hit without a head wind and in warmer temperatures. His anger clouded his judgment and told him to hit this shot harder than usual. So Jake took aim and spanked the ball with his six-iron about as hard as he could. As usual, he made solid contact, but the additional force and the slightly downward stroke Jake applied resulted in substantially more backspin than normal. Into the wind, the spin caused the ball to shoot up high into the air with a ballooning trajectory. The ball did make it over the water and just caught the front of the green. It took a high forward bounce when it landed, but on the second bounce it spun violently backwards toward the two men and the pond. Both men watched intently as the ball accelerated back down the false front of the green, down the grassy slope. They looked on as it slid pitifully into the water, startling a couple of nearby geese on its ignoble entry.

Jake barely controlled an overwhelming urge to helicopter his club into the lake after the ball. He had no choice but to hit three off the tee. Without any thought, he pulled a fresh ball out of his bag and ripped another swing. Fortunately, this time he stuck it about twenty feet left of the pin.

Once again, neither player spoke to one another as they walked toward the hole. The silence was deafening. This was becoming a very uncomfortable round for both players. Ken proceeded to splash his shot out of the greenside bunker to about six feet below the pin. Jake just missed his twenty-foot putt for bogie, and Ken gave him the comeback putt for a score of five on the par three. Ken sunk his putt for par and once again easily took the hole. Jake was already down three in the match after only three holes.

The pair continued playing their match throughout the challenging front nine, with virtually no conversation and even less camaraderie. Ken continued his steady if unspectacular play, while Jake, getting further and further behind, continually pushed his abilities to try to pull off ever more heroic shots.

After nine holes, Ken scored a handicap consistent 42, six shots over par. He was five up in the match and was never in doubt of losing a hole in the match throughout the front nine. Meanwhile, Jake had made several brutal scores and was having a miserable time. Unless Ken totally collapsed, which seemed unlikely given his steady style of play, it was apparent that Ken was going to easily win their eighteen-hole match.

Most importantly, Ken was disappointed as Jake was taking the match far too seriously and his attitude was spoiling what would likely be the last round of the season for both men. Ken felt badly for Jake and decided it was time to help him improve his score.

# CHAPTER 3
## THE TURNING POINT

# CHAPTER 3

Ken enjoyed competition and loved winning, but he also loved helping others to drive results, regardless of whether the game was golf, business or life. It was painfully obvious that Jake possessed exceptional talent and had tremendous ability. It was also absolutely clear to Ken that it was not Jake's lack of ability; rather, it was his philosophical and strategic approach to the game that wasn't quite up to par. Ken was one of those leaders who had the passion and heart to quickly sense a person's spirit and know how to help them redirect their energy into a more positive direction.

After the outward nine, they reached the turning point, the point where the holes began working their way back to the clubhouse. Situated at the far corner of the property was the halfway house, a picturesque log cabin where they could pick up a beverage and take a brief respite from the fall wind and bright, sparkling sunshine.

Ken leaned towards Jake and said, "You know Jake, the rest of this round isn't looking like it's going to be a lot of fun. How about we try playing a different kind of game? Even though I'm ahead by five holes, I'm willing to forfeit the match to you and buy you lunch after the round." Ken took a sip of his warm drink and continued, "However, you'll have to agree to play by my rules and follow my advice before each and every shot you play during the rest of the round. You know, you have significantly more talent, strength and ability than I do for this game, yet we sport the same handicap, and I'm whipping you in today's match. Your whole game plan is off. Your purpose, strategy and execution of the game need improvement. Your fundamentals, mechanics and shot talent are pretty darned solid, but your strategic approach really needs help. If you're prepared to accept my mentoring, then I'll forfeit our match and spring for our lunch."

Jake couldn't believe what he heard. They were halfway through the round, Ken was miles ahead in the match, and there seemed to be no reason for Ken to forfeit now! Jake spoke up to confirm what he heard. "You mean that you are willing to give me the match that I'm pretty much destined to lose, and all I have to do is to accept your advice during the rest of the round? How could I possibly say no?"

Jake knew about Ken and his reputation as a player with integrity and as great business leader. Normally, Jake was one of those competitive players whose ego wouldn't accept advice from anyone. He was smarter, tougher and far more capable than most of his contemporaries. However, Ken's offer was sincere, friendly and disarming. Anyway, being five down, Jake knew he was virtually certain to lose this match and couldn't pass up such a great offer and a free lunch!

"I don't have anything to lose. Sounds great!" Jake reached out and offered to shake Ken's hand.

"It's a deal then," Ken said as Jake accepted the offer and shook on it to confirm. "You win today's match. I'll buy you lunch and will stop playing my ball so I can coach you through the course for the final nine holes," Ken reiterated, shaking Jake's hand.

"You know," Ken smiled at Jake, "I remember when I was your age, I used to love to cream the ball and try to pull off the incredible shots, too. But until I learned my lesson, I too lost far too many balls and far too many matches until I took a more strategic approach to drive results. Before we begin," Ken continued, "we need to think about your reason for playing the game…your "purpose." I'd like you to consider why you play the game. What is your core reason for playing?"

Jake thought this a strange question to ask someone at the golf course, but he promised to play along with Ken and said, "Isn't the reason to compete in anything obvious? I play to win, to get the best possible score and to defeat the competition."

"Is that all?" Questioned Ken.

Jake thought a bit more about this question. "It's been a long time since I've thought about that. I was just a teenager when I started playing. We used to have tons of fun just whacking the heck out of all the old balls we could get our hands on. We'd go to the park or to the local driving range and try to hit them high, low, left, right, hard and soft. It was great fun just to make contact and see the ball fly through the air. When we finally got the hang of it, being able to launch the ball high in the air was like we were flying ourselves. It was like freedom."

"So think about why you really play the game today," Ken said. "What is your higher level reason or purpose today?"

Jake was quiet and thoughtful for a couple of moments. It was clear that he hadn't really considered what his philosophical purpose for playing the game was for quite some time. Finally he looked over towards Ken and said with a sense of calm, "The reason or purpose I play golf is to enjoy the game. That's it. My purpose for playing golf is to have fun and enjoy the game."

"Did you enjoy the game on the front nine?" queried Ken.

"No," Jake replied honestly. "I was angry at the game and frustrated with myself. I don't like losing. It wasn't much fun at all."

"Okay," said Ken. "Let's change that right now. From now on, you agree to enjoy the game, whatever happens. Agreed?"

"Agreed!" replied Jake.

"Great!" Said Ken. "Let's head out to the tenth tee and go have some fun."

# CHAPTER 4
## THE INWARD NINE

# CHAPTER 4

The tenth hole was a 500-yard, narrow and straight ahead par five. On the left side was a long fairway bunker that would catch most errant drives heading left. Farther left it was out of bounds all the way up to the green. The right hand rough wasn't too thick, and there was a sprinkling of trees along the right side. The wind was steady, and the hole was playing straight downwind. For longer, powerful players like Jake, this hole was quite reachable in two strokes today.

"Now, the game is about three things: purpose, strategy and execution. By focusing on these three things, you will improve your results," Ken reiterated.

Jake repeated, "Purpose, strategy, and execution. Got it."

"Okay," Ken continued, "first, we have agreed that your purpose for playing is to enjoy the game, right?" He confirmed without waiting for the reply. "So, whatever happens, good, bad or ugly, you will enjoy the game, right?"

"Right," confirmed Jake.

"Now, onto strategy and then execution. Our next step is to determine your optimal strategy, given your capabilities and the external environment," Ken mentored. "A strategic approach requires that you apply a consistent analytical method that you follow with discipline before each and every round, before each and every hole, and before each and every shot.

"The first step in strategy is to conduct an evaluation of the external environment to monitor the conditions of the course, the hole, the weather, the wind, your lie and the competition. Secondly, you must accurately determine your abilities, strengths, weaknesses, faults and limitations to play the game."

Ken leaned up against a grand old oak tree and wisely continued. "Now, I've been a member at this course for more years than I care to mention, and I have probably hit a shot from every square inch of the turf in almost every weather condition. This gives me some solid insight into our environment. Also, I've been watching your swing over the last nine holes and have a pretty fair idea about the strengths and weaknesses of your game at the physical, mental and spiritual levels. Considering your own capabilities and the external environment into account, perhaps you could tell me what your game plan is for this hole?"

"Well, it's obvious," Jake said as he reached into his bag. "It's a very reachable par five. I'll just whip out my driver and fire one right down the middle. If I catch it right, then I can probably get a mid iron onto the green and have a putt for eagle!" Jake pointed down the fairway with his driver in hand.

"Have you been listening?" Ken said feigning annoyance due to the lack of real strategic thinking by his new pupil. "Put that club back in your bag. What'll happen if you spray your driver on this narrow hole like you did on most of the preceding holes we've just played?"

Jake was silent.

"If you hit your driver and try to blast it down the fairway on this hole, you have three likely outcomes. Yes, you could hit it pure straight down the gut, or you could also spray it just a bit either left or right on this narrow hole. If you play the driver and you head right, you'll probably miss the fairway and end up in the rough or possibly in the trees. On the left, you'll flirt with the fairway bunker or worse, if you hit a high snapping hook that clears the bunker, you'll end up going out of bounds. Only one of those options leaves you with a sound result, the other two would likely lead at best to a par, possibly a bogey, or perhaps even worse."

"What do you advise?" Jake acquiesced.

"Well, with it being downwind, I suggest you pull out your three wood. I've seen you hit your three-wood, and like most players, you have significantly greater accuracy and consistency with it, especially if you hit your natural draw. Also, given that this shot is directly down-wind, it's highly likely that a reasonably well struck three wood with a naturally higher ball flight than a driver would result in the wind, carrying it just as far as a well struck driver would anyway."

Ken stood behind the tee and pointed down the fairway. "Now, you should tee up your ball on the left side of the blocks, aim down the right edge of the fairway, and do your best to play your natural draw. This simple technique of using the tee blocks more strategically opens up the fairway, helps takes away one side of the course, and allows for a significantly higher margin of error. Anyway you look at it, the likely probability of making a successful outcome with your three wood is strategically many times greater than using your driver, while taking significantly less risk!"

"But it's not as enjoyable hitting the three wood as it is hitting the driver," Jake pleaded.

"Do you enjoy blasting your driver out of bounds or deep into the woods?" Ken asked rhetorically. "Of course not! Besides, you agreed to do what I advised, so here's your three wood. Now, place your tee on the left side of the blocks and tee it low to the ground so that you'll reduce the chances of hitting a hard snapping hook. Remember, your strategy will be to focus your initial path to start out toward the right edge of the fairway and play your natural draw."

"So what's your thinking behind this approach?" asked Jake.

"Well, one of the world's greatest strategists taught me that the consistently best approach to obtain a winning result is to take a conservative strategic aim and to execute aggressively," Ken explained.

"Hmmm. That's interesting," Jake said, looking forward to an aggressive swing.

"Now, about execution," Ken explained. "Execution in the game needs to be uncontrolled and automatic. To achieve excellence in execution in golf, business or life for that matter, it is necessary to unleash the power of your mind. Commitment to excellence is key. The key to working towards excellence lies in your subconscious mind. This is the part of your brain that is the control center for automatic performance. In golf, it is virtually impossible to consciously control the 327 or more mechanical activities required for an absolutely, positively, perfectly correct golf swing that takes less than a couple of seconds to perform. The only way to achieve solid execution is to surrender control of the outcome to the subconscious mind."

Ken went on to explain to Jake, "The subconscious mind is the part of your brain that controls your automatic responses and allows you to produce a great golf swing. Anyone can use the following technique to improve the results through subconscious programming. The power of your subconscious mind to pre-program your golf shots will improve your likelihood of success."

"Really?" Jake questioned.

"Yes. Before each and every shot, you must stand behind the ball and clearly imagine the outcome you desire," Ken described. "Not only must you see the desired outcome, you must engage your conscious mind to truly visualize, hear, feel, believe and, ideally, know that the outcome you desire will occur. It is very important to engage all of your senses to visualize the outcome you desire through the power of your conscious mind. We all have a significant degree of control over our conscious mind. We can make our conscious mind create a preview of the outcome that we intend to occur and engrave that image into the subconscious. The more real this preview is, the greater the likelihood of turning your preview into reality. You must not only envision the shot, you need to go further. You must actually feel the swing, imagine you hear the sound of crisp impact, and, ideally, even experience the positive feeling you desire after the shot prior to actually making it occur!"

Ken went on, "So once you have successfully previewed the vision of the future, you are then ready to address the ball and move into the next step, which is to allow the outcome to occur. When you address the ball, allow your total being to focus simultaneously on the target, the outcome you desire, and your swing path through the ball. You must grasp hold of all of these thoughts in your essence simultaneously, firmly with positive energy and determination, but without any negative force."

"OK, I'll give it a go," Jake said, taking a practice swing.

"That's the spirit, Jake. Now, it's time to execute your swing. In order to execute well, you must let go of control, while at the same time, remaining in control of the outcome. This is a yin and yang kind of activity. You allow your previewed outcome to occur, believing that it will occur, trusting in the result, and absolutely knowing that it will happen. You must release conscious control over the effort, while knowing that you will achieve the result. Once you have reached this almost meditative state, you can allow your subconscious mind to perform the physical activity that you have preprogrammed into it to perform."

Ken started to see a glimpse of understanding in Jake's eyes. Ken knew that during a swing, a player allows the motion to occur physically while the mind remains free of any negative emotions or excessively strong positive ones. Ken was hoping to teach Jake that the optimal state of mind was a calm, positive, determined, knowing attitude with a sense of play.

Ken continued, "After your shot, if you produce the outcome you previewed or reasonably close to it, then immediately reinforce the result by positively rewarding yourself through a positive emotional compliment, either internally or externally, but do it quietly; otherwise, your playing partners might resent your behavior. If you hit a bad shot, which we all do, you must either minimize or eliminate any negative emotions, as this will only give it more energy and increase the likelihood of a negative occurrence in the future."

"Wow!" said Jake, wondering whether he had just signed up to join a brainwashing cult. "I've never heard anything quite that deep about a golf swing before. Almost everything I have ever learned has been about the mechanics of the game. And I need to do that before every shot?"

"You do if you want to play to your potential," said Ken. "It's good that no one is on the course today, so we can take our time. I'll walk you through it again."

Ken walked Jake through the thinking once again, slowly and step by step so that Jake comprehended it clearly. "It seems that you understand this concept. Now it's time for you to allow your results to occur."

Jake then stood behind the ball and did his best to visualize the preview and really "feel" his outcome. He felt a bit awkward at first, but with no one else, around he felt very comfortable with

Ken's calming presence. He did his best to get into the spirit of the game. Once Jake's visualization and feeling was internalized, he addressed the ball, took aim down the right side and then simply allowed his swing to occur.

It was the first time in recent memory that Jake didn't try to force his shot to happen. It was a very relaxed and enjoyable feeling. For the first time in years, Jake swung without feeling fear, anger, anxiety, tension or nervousness.

The ball sprang off the club effortlessly. It flew directly down his chosen target line. The ball hooked a bit more than Jake had previewed, but thanks to the downward blowing wind, his ball managed to fly reasonably straight and pretty darn far. It ended up stopping on the first cut of rough on the left side about 220 yards away from the center of the green. From this vantage point, Jake had a clear shot directly downwind to the green.

"Great shot!" said Ken. "You stayed on purpose. Your strategy was sound, and your execution was reasonably good, especially for a first attempt. Now you're in a great position to go for the green!"

Ken went on as the pair walked toward Jake's ball: "Between shots, try your best to enjoy the scenery. It's a spectacular day, we are playing an awesome game, we live in one of the world's greatest countries on a spectacular planet, and we're having a wonderful experience," Ken said. "Our lives here on planet Earth goes by far too quickly, and we all must learn to both appreciate and enjoy each and every moment of our existence." He philosophized as only someone closer to the end of his own life could. "It's all part of enjoying the game."

Interestingly, Jake's expression had seemingly begun to transform from his earlier anger and darkness towards adopting a much more positive, tranquil state of being.

As they approached the ball Ken continued, "Now let's analyze the situation so we can once again determine your optimal strategy. We are still playing directly downwind. It is about 220 yards to the center of the green, and the pin is on the left edge of a pretty level green. There is a large bunker well short and left of the green that will only come into play if you totally miss your shot from here. As you can see, there is another nasty little pot bunker that is short right of the green to catch a short, bailout fade. The terrain left of the green slopes sharply downhill and leads to the out of bounds stakes further left. No matter what happens, we don't want to end up anywhere near the left side of the green, even though the pin is there. The risk is far too high to go anywhere near it."

Ken had learned to look well beyond where the pin is placed and to survey further afield. Strategic players adopt a wider view and examine the larger territory to allow him greater perspective. He knew that golf course architects are clever masochists who love to torture players. They know most people tend to overestimate their ability and choose the wrong club that usually results in ending up short of the hole. Therefore, the architects tend to put many of the stroke-eating hazards in the front of the green. Strategic players survey the entire environment before determining their optimal shot.

"Judging by your past behavior, from here you would probably have taken aim at the middle of the green and try to draw the ball back just right of the pin to go for an eagle, right?" Ken asked.

"Yeah," said Jake proudly, "that's what I usually try to do on this hole if I hit a good tee shot."

"Now, if you were a Tour player, then that's what I would advise. They have spent years honing their skills, are very precise players, and have a much higher expected success rate than we amateurs. Unfortunately, we don't have the same level of consistency with our misses and need to be much more conservative in our chosen strategy if we expect to improve our score."

Ken pointed down the fairway. "Strategically, with your natural draw, you should aim several yards off the right edge of the green and hit a club that will likely result in your risking being a bit long and right of the green. You likely won't end up with a makeable eagle putt, but if you play it far enough right, you'll have a good chance at a birdie and an excellent shot at a par. Remember, the best players make very few birdies during a round, and even the greatest in the world rarely make eagles. But the players who make the most out of their game are the ones that minimize their bogies or scores that are worse."

Ken explained, "It's not how good your good shots are; it's how good your misses are that matters. Whenever possible, do your best to aim away from hazards in the game that eat up valuable strokes. Remember…aim conservatively and swing aggressively. With the wind behind us, the hole is playing about 200 yards," he continued. "Considering these conditions, your ability to make solid impact, and your power, you can probably hit your four-iron around 210 to 220 yards. Even if you miss- hit the ball somewhat, it should easily clear the nasty pot bunker, which is about 180 yards away on the short right side of the green. As a result, your target is directly over that bunker to the back right first cut of the green. Ignore the actual pin and pretend that there is an imaginary target that's shaped just like a bull's-eye that is just on the far back right edge of the green. Now that bull's-eye is your target."

Jake raised a skeptical brow.

Ken smiled, "Remember you promised that you would do what I asked, okay?"

"Okay," Jake said grudgingly, reluctantly letting go of his dream of scoring an eagle.

"Now, stand behind the shot and run your preview. Let yourself see and feel the shot; allow yourself to sense the positive emotion you want to experience after the shot before you actually make your swing. When you are ready, pick an intermediate target a foot or two ahead of your ball, and then square up your stance to that spot. Take one last look at your imaginary bull's-eye, focus on the ball, and then let the swing happen," Ken instructed.

Jake went through this new routine. He previewed the shot imagining his natural modest draw starting right of the green and drifting back to the back right corner of the green toward his imaginary bull's-eye. He then set up for the real thing, freed his mind, and allowed it to occur. Jake made a great flowing swing and really flushed it. The ball flew away as aimed. However, it didn't have any draw spin on it this time and ended up flying pretty much dead straight. The ball landed a few yards back and long of the green on the upslope behind the green. The ball stopped where it landed about five yards behind the green and about fifty feet from the pin.

"Excellent shot!" said Ken.

"What do you mean?" cried Jake. "It went too far and didn't draw. That ball's well off the green and nowhere near the pin!"

"Correct, but from where you are, at worst you'll likely make par and you have a darn good shot at birdie. If you had that opportunity on every hole, your handicap would be scratch or better!" Ken said excitedly.

"Did you know that even the greatest players in the world only make three or four swings a round that produce a shot exactly like they envisioned them? That means that the rest of their shots are misses! If on average, they make only three or four out of approximately thirty-six to maybe forty full swings in a round, then they are only batting around ten percent. That means about ninety percent of their shots are misses! What any good and all the great players do really well is to be strategic about their abilities and manage their game and their misses extremely well."

Jake had executed a reasonable shot that gave him a solid chance at a good score on this hole. More importantly, the miss took him away from all of the trouble that could lead to bogey, a double bogey or worse. On this hole he had taken two swings, both of which were not really his best or exactly what he had envisioned. In both cases, he ended up in good shape primarily due to coming up with and sticking to a sound strategy, not due to exceptional shot making. Jake and Ken walked up and around to the back of the green and surveyed the territory below.

"So, after two less than perfect swings, here we are at the back of the green in two on a par five. You're fortunate that you possess such great power, as most players would love to have your prowess. We're about five yards off the green, with a downhill lie to a pretty flat green. The ball is sitting down in the grass pretty well and will probably run out hard and low. Take out a pitching wedge and hit the shot with a steady, wrist-free swing just like you would with a putt. Ensure you keep your hands ahead of the club head throughout the chip, and have your shot land a few yards on the green and run out to the hole," Ken advised Jake.

"But," Jake began, "Wouldn't taking a big cut with an open faced lob wedge like the pros do give me a better chance at getting it tight to the pin?"

"Yes, it would, but a shot like that is also extremely risky as it gives you a much higher probability of either chili-dipping it short or worse, blading it over the green and possibly even out of bounds!

The better strategy is the one that will result in the best average expected outcome for your ability level, not what you can achieve on your best shot. That calls for you to just get it on the green with a certain two putt for par and a possible chance at a birdie."

"Well, if you insist," said Jake.

"I do," confirmed Ken.

Jake once again went through his new routine. He previewed the shot, practiced it and then took his stance. He took the club back just fine, but then dipped his shoulder down a bit and stubbed it badly. The ball barely made it onto the green and rolled to about fifteen feet from the pin.

"Damn!" cursed Jake.

"Hey, you promised to enjoy the game and not to express any negative emotions after a disappointing shot!" Ken reminded. "Besides, even though you totally flubbed that shot, you can still make a birdie or par from where you are! Now, let's look at the putt. First of all, did you know that Dave Pelz, the great short game guru, has scientifically determined that most amateurs under-read the break by two or even three times the actual amount! Even the elite players he tested almost always under-read the amount of break. Secondly, he also determined that the optimal energy required to regularly sink putts is to give it enough speed, so that if it misses the cup, it'll travel eighteen inches past the hole. So, whenever you putt, double the break that you think you see and then focus on hitting the ball so that it would roll about eighteen inches past the hole. Most players get so overly focused on reading the break and don't invest enough thought focusing on the weight. Focusing more energy on the weight required is more likely to lead to a better outcome."

Jake and Ken both read the putt and agreed on the amount of break they saw, and then they doubled it. Just as importantly, they assessed the required energy to get the ball to finish up eighteen inches past the hole. Ken made sure that Jake quickly surveyed his putt from behind, from the side, and from the opposite side of the hole. This quick evaluation allowed Jake's body to internalize the distance and slope of the green so that he could evaluate the proper weight. Jake previewed his putt and stroked through the ball reasonably well, but pushed it a hair. It just burned the right edge and ended up barely past the hole. Jake tapped it in easily for his par.

"Great work, Jake. Now, let's look back at this hole and do a quick debrief of your purpose, strategy, and execution. You did stay pretty positive and seemed to enjoy the game, so that's a great start. We developed a sound strategy, and even though you didn't really execute the shots exactly like you had intended, you still made a par! See what a difference having an appropriate strategy makes. You can still earn a solid score, even when you aren't playing your best. Just think what'll happen when you hit some of the shots that you are capable of producing! Alright, let's head out the eleventh hole and see what we can do."

The eleventh was a stunning 380-yard valley hole. The tees were elevated, and the fairway dropped down below with three prickly fairway bunkers. These bunkers came from the left side of the rough almost into the center of the short grass. Ahead of the bunkers, the left side was extremely wide open. On the right side, just a few yards off the edge of the fairway, there was a dense ravine that was a graveyard for hundreds of golf balls. The green up ahead was quite large and loomed sharply above the valley fairway down below. Wind was not a factor as the tree lined valley permitted very little of it to come into play.

"Now I know you have a solid ability to make solid contact and consistently hit powerful drives. However, you do have a tendency to be a bit wild and end up either left or right. On many holes, you'll have to discipline yourself to use less club, but on holes like this one, your best strategy may be to take out your driver and let it rip. As you can clearly see, the fairway is wide open past the three bunkers. Although the accuracy you have isn't always the best, you do generally make solid contact and are highly consistent when it comes to distance. Given this fact, making a solid drive should fly the ball over the bunkers to the generous fairway beyond and this should leave you with a short iron into the green. So, on this hole, I think that your best strategic option with the least risk and the best average expected outcome is to take out your driver, aim for the middle of the fairway well over the bunkers and let it fly at around eighty to ninety percent of your full power."

Jake agreed with Ken's strategic analysis and was happy to blast away. He went through his new routine and was very comfortable with the preview feeling. He took his stance, aimed a bit left of center, and hammered the ball way down the fairway. The ball faded a bit to the right, but it was nowhere near the ravine on the far right edge. The ball was launched with enough energy to clear the bunkers as it took off on when it landed on the down slope of the bunkers and skidded directly down the fairway within the 100-yard marker. Jake, beaming, turned to look at his newfound coach.

"Great shot!" Ken complimented.

"Thanks," said Jake. The two men walked down to his ball. Jake needed just a gap wedge to reach the pin in the center of the green and looked to Ken for some advice.

"Now, my recommendation on any club less than a nine iron is to try to hit it straight. With a shorter, more controllable shaft length and increased loft of the clubface, you will have more control with significantly less sidespin generated, and it is the sidespin that causes the ball to curve. Making the ball spin clockwise is what will produce a left to right fade or slice, and a counterclockwise spin results in a right to left draw or hook, but the a higher lofted club will have significantly less spin and will tend to fly straighter." Ken reminded Jake.

"As far as aiming, it is generally best to aim towards the largest portion of the green and overcome the urge to go hunting the flag. If anything, you should generally aim on the opposite side of the pin. That way, you'll usually end up somewhere on or near the green and will rarely end on the short side of the green with a difficult chip to a tight pin," Ken continued.

Jake understood the wisdom in this approach and quietly agreed. The pin was on the left side of the green. Jake agreed that he should aim directly for the large center of the green. He went through his new routine and hit a high spinner that flew exactly as he envisioned, just right of the pin, and it spun back to about twenty feet from the cup, safely in the middle of the green.

The two men walked up the hill to the green where they went through the process to analyze the putt. Jake and Ken went through the putting analysis, and then Jake drained his side hill breaker for a birdie! Their love for the game and this performance was evident on both players' faces, and a positive field of energy now seemed to envelop the two-man team.

Jake played on, with the help of Ken's advice, to consecutively par the next three holes. He safely bogeyed the following two holes that played into the wind and then earned a par with a great up and down on the seventeenth. Jake was now just one over par on the back nine coming up to the eighteenth, a downwind par five dogleg right with a drive to a blind landing area.

Here, Jake was instructed by Ken once again to take a more conservative line aiming further left than Jake would have usually determined on his own. This more conservative strategy paid off as Jake ended up making a powerful shot that faded a bit, but thanks to Ken's aim adjustment, the ball just caught the far right edge of the fairway and bounced forward on the down slope of the hill and cruised well down the fairway, leaving Jake with only 220 yard downwind second shot to the uphill par five green ahead.

The pair walked over the hill and both smiled to one another as they saw Jake's ball sitting beautifully on the right edge of the fairway.

"So, have a look up ahead to the hole with a fresh perspective. Where is all of the trouble?" asked Ken.

Looking uphill towards the hole, Jake could clearly see that the bunkers, the rough short right, the trees on the left, and the false front dropping away from the green were all between them and the hole. He knew that the green was pretty much in a giant horseshoe shaped bowl and the landscaping around the back portion of the green all sloped back towards the green and the pin. The flag stood in attention in the center of the spacious green.

Jake looked back at Ken and said, "It doesn't seem like there's any major disadvantage being long. All of the major trouble is short of the hole. I guess my best option is to take an extra club, hit it smoothly and risk going a bit long. Normally, I would have hit my four-iron from here and hope to stiff it to the pin, but I think I'll take one more club with a risk that it could go a bit long. What do you think?" asked Jake.

"I think you've learned a great deal," said Ken. "From now on, you're on your own!"

Jake pulled out a three-iron. He took dead aim at the pin and relaxed, knowing he could safely veer either right or left. He previewed the shot, took his stance and then let it fly. In his eagerness, Jake looked up a bit prematurely, which caused him to pull up just a bit and hit the ball a bit low on the clubface. The thin shot lost some of its distance and started to drift right as thin shots do. Fortunately, since he had taken the extra club, it had enough power to make it to pin high. The ball hit hard on the side slope at the right side of the green, then kicked back towards the hole when the players lost sight of the ball because of the uphill angle.

They quietly walked up the hill and both men shared an appreciative glance when they saw Jake's ball resting about twenty five feet right of the final pin. Without speaking, Jake marked and cleaned his ball. He examined the line and took a cruise around the ball to survey the landscape, making sure that he took an extra moment to get a feel for the break, doubled it, and assessed the correct weight. He lined up his putt and took his stance. He felt great about this putt and committed himself to a smooth stroke as he relaxed and stayed firm while letting go of control. The ball left the putter on a great roll. It curved in a lazy arc and held its line barely enough to catch the bottom edge of the lip and drop into the cup...for an eagle!

Jake was ecstatic. He leaped up, threw his cap into the air, and let out a shout of joy. Amazingly, Jake had played the inward nine at one under par. This was his best score ever on nine holes and was a great accomplishment on some tough finishing holes. What a spectacular way to end the season!

Jake ran up to Ken and lifted him off the ground with a giant bear hug to thank him for his coaching and team work. Jake went on to excitedly say, "I know you forfeited our match and promised to pick up lunch, but thanks to your advice, this has been the best nine holes I have ever played. I've never played nine holes under par before. It would be unsportsmanlike for me to allow you to buy us lunch. Please, I insist that I treat you to lunch. Besides, I haven't used up my minimum yet for the rest of the season, and it would be a waste otherwise."

Ken happily agreed, and the gentlemen went for a quick shower and met again in the clubhouse for lunch.

# CHAPTER 5
## HOW LEADERS DRIVE RESULTS

# CHAPTER 5

Ken and Jake reconvened for their lunch. Fortunately, both men did not have any personal commitments until the evening and were free to share a leisurely afternoon meal together. Jake was grateful to Ken for sharing his insights about purpose, strategy and execution on the golf course. He truly enjoyed their inward nine together and was thrilled to have not only played exceptionally well, but to also have established a positive friendship with Ken. During their lunch, both men relived the shots of the day and shared some great laughs about their play together. When Ken asked Jake about his work activities, Jake turned somber.

"You know what it's like being the boss," he went on. "It can be very lonely. It's great when things are going well, but it's not very enjoyable when you have to carry the entire load all of the time."

"Yeah, I know," Ken said. "Leading a team can be a very lonely game sometimes. That's one of the reasons I love playing golf. It's a great escape and a chance to get outdoors, breathe some fresh air, break away from the responsibility of it all, and have some fun and relaxation with friends and colleagues. If it wasn't for golf, I don't think I would have been as successful as I have been. As a matter of fact, I know so. If it wasn't for the game of golf, I wouldn't have connected with the people and ideas that helped me transform our business team to become so successful."

"Really?" Jake wondered. "You know, I haven't been having such a great time in my business activities lately, and the poor results are spilling over and negatively impacting my personal life as well," he confessed. "Our business results have been lousy, the people who report to me haven't been performing very well, and I'm feeling frustrated and stressed, but am at a loss to improve results. Do you have any thoughts?"

"In my experience, the best way for a leader to drive results is to build, develop and grow a great team," said Ken.

"I know, I know," said Jake. "Getting great results from teamwork is what business is all about, and I'm looking for a better way to get them to perform at a higher level."

"Yes," said Ken, "enabling a team to perform at an exceptional level is possibly the greatest challenge any real leader faces."

"I agree, I agree," replied Jake. "I hire good people, I pay them well, I treat them with respect, and I give them sound direction. Nevertheless, I don't get the results from the business that I know we are capable of achieving."

"I faced the same challenges several years ago," said Ken. "You need to work on your team's purpose, strategy and execution. The approach that worked so well for you in your golf game today also works unbelievably well to improve your score in the game of business and can even help you in your personal life as well."

"Really? How can I do that?" Jake asked.

Ken said, "All successful leaders somehow ensure that their team is on purpose, that they develop a great winning strategy, and that they regularly execute the team's game plan. I learned many years ago that the best approach to produce exceptional performance is to foster team spirit, and that spirit must come from the passion and power that lies within each and every player."

"How did you do that?" Jake asked.

"Well, there are numerous contributing factors. I believe that any great leader must demonstrate a sincere love for the game that he plays. It will be this passion that allows him to overcome the challenges he will face in the game. He must lead with courage, integrity, and honesty. Any ethical or moral dilemmas must be resolved fairly and quickly by the leader. He must develop and communicate a great vision with the involvement of his team. And perhaps, most importantly, he must inspire, motivate, and drive his team members to become exceptional players that continually strive to play their individual and collective games at the highest possible level," Ken expressed.

"I see," said Jake. "I am pretty passionate about my work, and I do my best to personally perform at the highest possible level. However, I seem to have challenges getting my team to be as passionate and committed to achieving the goals as I am. I do my best to tell them how to achieve results at the level I would like them to and know they are capable of. Any thoughts?"

"Well," said Ken knowingly, "several years ago, I was in a similar situation. Our business had great potential, but we weren't really performing very well. I was working long hard hours and felt like I was carrying the weight of the world on my shoulders. As a result, I was getting frustrated and angry and was really spinning my wheels. Work was tough, my golf game was taking a real beating, my personal life was suffering, and life was starting to get me down. I knew I needed some help to turn things around."

"Yeah, I know exactly how you feel," Jake commiserated.

"So I went out and hired some high priced strategy consultants with great credentials to help me out. They interviewed our business team, ripped the company information apart, and then went away for several few weeks to analyze our data, all the while billing me on an expensive daily basis. Then they returned with the fruits of their labors with all kinds of high-level analysis, charts, graphs and strategies. They proceeded to tell us what we needed to do, what our performance measures should be, and how we needed to behave. They packed up their gear and left us with a bunch of papers and a great big fat bill. Unfortunately, their advice and recommendations never really panned out. Our team never executed," Ken said.

"Yeah, I've gone down that road, too. Those guys are really intelligent and talented. Their ideas sound great and seem to make sense, but they never really seem to take hold," Jake confirmed.

"After going through a couple of rounds of working with these kinds of advisors, our team morale was getting really low, and we continued to under perform. Our results were weak and seemed to be getting worse by the day. It was then, at pretty much the lowest point in my business career, that I attended a charity golf tournament where I met a guy who helped me transform my game," Ken recollected.

"Oh yeah?" Jake perked up.

"Yeah, it was one of those corporate charity golf events where they get you to network by mixing the players up and creating foursomes of people who don't know one another," Ken said. "The tournament format was a team scramble, where all of the foursomes play together as a team. In this format, everyone takes a shot from the tee. Then the team selects the best one, and everyone take turns hitting their next shot from the same spot. The team continues playing out the hole this way, even on the putting green until the team holes out. You play as a team and have one collective team score that can get pretty darned low. It is a great format for charity and business golf events since it allows players of all abilities to enjoy the game together."

"I've played in that format before. It can be a lot of fun, especially if you hook up with a good group," Jake nodded.

"You're right there. Our foursome decided that our lowest handicap golfer should be the team captain," Ken reminisced. "Well, his leadership style on the golf course was very positive, friendly, involving and collaborative, yet firm under pressure. From the quality of his shots, you could immediately tell that he was a solid player, but perhaps even more importantly, it seemed that he was able to get all of the other players to really get into the game and participate at their highest level.

"He initially shared a couple of jokes to get everyone comfortable and at ease with one another. He then did a quick assessment of each of our playing strengths and weaknesses on the course. He was quickly able to get all of us to open up and feel comfortable to share information about ourselves and about playing with one another. He inspired all of us to enjoy the game and to play with positive determination and confidence.

"In no time at all, it was like we were long-term committed team members. His knowledge of the game, his ability to read people, and his approach to involving everyone got us all really enthused about the opportunity to play together. Most importantly, he got everyone on the team into developing and executing the golfing strategy for the entire team. We all collaborated to determine what shot we should hit, the clubs we should use, in what order we should play, where we should aim and how we should all play together. We cheered one another's successes and supported each other when someone didn't perform to their potential. It turned out to be a great team effort and a heck of a lot of fun."

"It sounds like it was a good day," Jake said.

"It was an exceptional day! The weather was perfect; we all had a great time, and the team played unbelievably well. The chemistry of our team was amazing. In almost no time, we were in sync with one another, had lots of laughs together, and really got focused on our team game. Everyone contributed by making some incredible shots. We had a couple of lucky breaks, and wouldn't you know it, even the least experienced player on the team sunk a couple of big putts to make some birdies. We ended up having the lowest team score and won the tournament. We all donated our prizes back to the charity and helped raise the most funds they had ever earned for their important cause," Ken smiled.

"It feels great when you win and give something back to help others," Jake said positively.

"After the round during dinner, I asked our golf team captain what he did to earn his living. He informed me that he had developed a unique team performance program to help leaders drive results. He worked with various leadership teams to implement a comprehensive approach to help their teams develop and execute winning strategic plans," Ken recalled.

"And then what?" Jake led Ken on.

"He shared some insights about the three pillars of integrated strategic planning that form the foundation to develop and execute a successful business strategy," Ken said. "The first pillar is to continually research, interview, and understand your customers so that you understand their wants, needs and their buyer behavior. Every good venture needs to know what the customers need and how the competitors are positioned relative to one another from the customer's perspective.

"The second pillar is to ensure the team works passionately together in order to come up with its own effective strategy to grow the business to meet those needs. Unlike the management consultants we had previously paid some big bucks for, it turns out that it is imperative that the operating team needed to be the strategic experts and not some outsiders. The team had to develop the game plan both from the outside in and from the inside out. Just like the approach that worked so well for our golf team at the charity golf event, getting team members to get positively engaged in the development of their own game plan and actions is what really drives results.

"Finally, the third pillar is to ensure on an ongoing basis that the leader has a process in place to assess, recruit, retain and develop the best possible team of people playing the right positions who are continually striving to work together as a high performance team to achieve the team's common goals."

"Hmmm. Those are some pretty interesting insights. What did you do next?" Jake questioned.

"Well, as you can well appreciate, I really wanted to drive some exceptional business results in my own business and was quite eager to make things happen. Leaders like you and I tend to be very powerful people who are highly goal oriented. The vast majority of leaders tend to score very high in dominance, a critical behavior required to produce results.

"However, many of the people that we lead will have a very different mix of interests, talents and strengths. A great team always needs a mix of people with a variety of behaviors to function optimally. Some team members need to be strong influencers or more people-oriented, while some need to be very steady or systematic, and others need to be highly compliant or process oriented. The leader needs to mix and match the various personality types in order to architect the development of a cohesive team that will be consistent with the market needs, the competitive positioning, the team's own desires and then, most importantly, must ensure that everyone is working together.

"It is our job as the leader to pull together and manage team members and get them to continually strive to do and be their best. This requires a tremendous amount of people-knowledge and understanding. Unfortunately, sometimes the highly dominant personality naturally inherent within a leader will, in many cases, conflict with the some of the innate people skills and human psychology requirements needed to assess, architect, build, and maintain a great team."

"That is a conundrum, isn't it?" Jake wondered aloud as he sipped on his coffee.

"Exactly. As you know, to achieve business goals, we leaders need to work with and through people. This can be a very challenging activity for dominant people like ourselves, and we can benefit from some additional unbiased expertise that has experience helping other leaders build high performance teams.

"The guy I met at the charity golf event seemed like a trustworthy person with a good track record. He had some sound insights and had already demonstrated his talent and ability to get our team to work together on the golf course. I arranged for him to customize a team strategic planning program to see if it would work for me and my team," Ken explained.

"How did it work out?" Jake asked.

"The approach we undertook was initially very challenging. It involved ensuring that all three pillars to develop and execute our strategy were put into place: We embarked on a regular, ongoing process to do some quality market research. We actively conducted regular team-based strategic planning sessions. And, we continually worked together to assess, monitor, and build our cast of operating team members.

"It involved a substantial investment of our time and energy. However, it turned out to be a revelation for our business and ultimately, it was the key that unlocked the power of our team and drove results!" Ken offered. "Our profits went up, our sales went up, our employee satisfaction went up, I worked less, and my golf handicap went down!"

"That's great!" Jake said enviously.

"Yeah," said Ken. "The strategic team planning program really did work for us. To this day, we continue to apply an ongoing process that improves our team performance and drives business results. I sincerely believe that every business team should invest in this kind of activity and makebudget allowances for it. If all companies did this, I bet that they would be much more profitable and would all be much better places for people to work at. When I pioneered this outsourced activity, it was a bit revolutionary and may have been viewed by some as a leadership weakness. Fortunately, it has proven to be a tremendous strength and has become much more commonplace within advanced organizations."

"That's very interesting! But of course, you were savvy enough to realize the potential benefits. What do you think are the optimal qualities for this kind of relationship?" Jake asked.

"Ideally, you want a relationship with strategic leadership advisor that you might almost consider as a partner in your leadership role. Secondly, you'd like someone who has seen and worked with a wide range of cultures and organizations. Sometimes, working within one company and within one industry can get pretty narrow. A second set of eyes with a broader perspective can bring insights and ideas to implement that you'd never think of. You want someone with a sound educational background and experience working with a wide variety of companies ranging from large blue chip corporate firms to early stage entrepreneurial and technology ventures."

Ken went on, "They should also have experience working with a wide variety of cultures and with a wide variety of organizations, including private businesses, public companies, venture backed entities, not for profits, charitable organizations and even government groups. Having experience in a broad range of markets and situations is invaluable in helping you guide your team to perform. Ideally, they should also have experience in integrating mergers, in turnaround situations, with high growth ventures, with partnership disputes and more. You never know what the future will bring.

"Finally, and perhaps most importantly, they must be highly trusted and have a powerful ability to form strong relationships at all levels quickly. They need to be strong enough to lead and emotionally intelligent enough to help others flourish."

"Sounds like a pretty rare resource to find," Jake responded. "What else?"

"You need someone who's a marketer, a creative coach, a facilitator, a psychologist, a motivator and a strategist who is willing to challenge you, while at the same time, look out for your best interests. They need to know your business pretty well and must be a highly trusted sounding board for both you and your team," Ken instructed. "If possible, you want someone who can incorporate sound business knowledge, psychological assessments, organizational structuring talent, financial understanding, subconscious programming insights, sales expertise and marketing research capabilities to ensure you achieve your business goals."

"That sounds like a handful. So what are the real benefits?" Jake asked.

"Teamwork. It's all about producing high performance teamwork. And it's focused teamwork that turns into profit. We have found that a driven, focused team is the most powerful force in business. The true power of a team emanates from trust, passion and talent. Real teamwork harmonizes the collective spirit and focuses it on achieving a common, agreed up business outcome," Ken outlined. "In order for a leader to tap into the power of a team, he must first enable each one of his team members to self determine what truly motivates them individually before they can truly transform into a high performance team."

"OK, I think I get it," Jake said. "Can you tell me specifically about how you did it?"

"Well," Ken advised, "as you know, one of the most important roles of a leader is to find, attract, recruit and retain the best possible team of players. Ideally, your team members have the right balance of passion, talent and experience to play the game. Then, the leader is responsible to ensure that their team of players achieves alignment around purpose, strategy, and execution.

"Just like in your golf game today, a very important step for both the individual and the business team is to determine the individual and collective purpose. In order for a leader, his team, and a business to be aligned, there must be a shared philosophical purpose for them to collectively pursue with passion," Ken said.

"Yeah, yeah, yeah," said Jake. "I've heard all about this stuff. This is where corporate fat cats sit around and spend hours wasting time talking about mission, vision and values while burning up their shareholders resources. I have heard that this is a big fat waste of time."

"You're right. It can be a huge waste of time, effort and money if it's done badly. But, when it is done properly, it is an extremely powerful unifying force that binds under-performing groups of individuals into high performance teams," Ken countered. "Unfortunately, many leaders make a huge mistake by trying to assemble their team members to come up with a company mission, vision and values, before the leader and all of their team has done the internal work personally for themselves. Without this effort, the individuals on the team will never be truly able to be in alignment and will likely be skeptical of the purpose statements for the business and the leader's rationale for coming up with one. That's why the leader must ensure that his senior team members and, ideally, the entire company should go through a confidential personal process first that allows them to develop their own higher purpose for their lives and careers.

"In order for a team to realize its best performance, a few things need to be orchestrated. First of all, the individuals on the team must have the talent and experience required to do the job. Secondly and perhaps more importantly, the team members must personally possess the heart, the passion, the motivation and the spirit to achieve great results," Ken continued.

"You mean I have to be a spiritual leader as well?" Jake protested. "Gee, I thought my job was to be a business leader. Isn't spirit the job of people in the clergy?"

"Perhaps," said Ken. "Or, perhaps building great team spirit is one of the primary responsibilities of any true leader. How many great sports team have you seen that possess awesome talent but don't seem to possess much heart? Where do they end up? Usually they finish in the cellar. And how many teams have you seen that have far lesser talent that go on to win their division because they possess incredible passion for their game. The teams with spirit are the ones who win championships!

"Business is more of the same. There are tons of teams with players who have tremendous talent and potential who don't produce any real results. And you know what, I fault their leaders for this failure. The number one priority of any leader to get the team they lead to identify what they love to do, what they are passionate about, what they are here to do and then empower them to do it!

"A leader's role is to assemble a team of individuals with varying, but complementary talents and experiences who share a common passion and work with them in order to align their common energy or spirit into a powerful, unified, focused field of energy that will become greater than the sum of all of the individual parts combined. On an ongoing basis, the leader's role is to continually ensure that the team's energy is focused, on track and working towards achieving goals that will lead to the accomplishment of real activities that contribute to both the team's and the individual's common spirit. That is the true work of a leader," Ken mentored.

"You mean," Jake began slowly, "when a leader invests in helping the individuals on his team get on purpose with all of those that he leads, then the leader is truly maximizing their human potential, and that is what drives exceptional business performance to produce financial results?"

"Exactly!" Ken confirmed. "A company needs to define its purpose. A lot of firms use the terms mission, vision and values to cover this purpose or area of philosophy. Of course, you can use any terminology that makes sense to you and your team. A company's purpose or mission could be described as the reason for being. A vision is a clear, brief statement of a near term future view of the enterprise. Values are the common, agreed upon behaviors that the individual or group strives to adhere to and live by. Once again, these definitions apply equally well for individuals, for a team and for an organization. It is my sincere belief that the leader needs to ensure that the team members do this work personally before they attempt to develop their purpose which can be defined as the mission, vision, values for the enterprise."

"But I'm in the alternative energy technology game, not in the human potential business. I'm not trained to be a philosophical or spiritual leader," countered Jake. "I'm more like a general who leads by example, to know about my industry, to keep on top of various technologies, to drive the team and monitor its progress. And sometimes I have to give orders and discipline team members when required, to manage our finances and investor relations, to provide products and services as efficiently as possible, to get more customers and on and on and on. You see, I can't possibly take care of all of those other things while also being a philosophical or even spiritual advisor to my team."

"That may be true," said Ken. "The life of a leader is extremely complex, multi-faceted and getting even more complicated all the time. Perhaps that's why you might benefit from having another qualified player become part of your ongoing leadership process. Think for a moment about the world's best golfers. Not so long ago, all a player might have had was a golf swing coach. Now, each and every elite and aspiring player have swing coaches, fitness trainers, psychology coaches, financial advisors, and sports agents.

"Think of any professional or college sports team, and you'll see that they all have the head coach who, like yourself, leads their team. In addition, though, the head coach has an entire coaching staff with trainers, fitness coaches, strategy coaches and more who all fulfill various roles in the development, strategy, and growth of the team. In your business leadership team, you may best be served by a variety of leadership skill sets applied on an ongoing and consistent basis in order to ensure that your team is aligned, focused and on track," Ken explained.

"I see. So the idea is to in-source the management of some of our leadership activities to an expert, just like we out-source our payroll activities," Jake mused.

"That's right. Then, once the team has developed its purpose, a team needs to formulate its strategy. Just like we did during your golf round earlier today, developing a strategy is an ongoing, continuous process that entails working through a disciplined process with external information and input from the team."

"What do you think is the best way to develop a company strategy?" Quizzed an eager Jake.

"We have found that holding an annual two or three day strategic planning offsite with full-day quarterly reviews produces a great result," Ken shared confidently. "We usually get everyone together at intimate places with lots of natural beauty and good food and sometimes entertainment. We generally travel to a variety of nearby golf, ski and spa retreats. This way we can all do our planning in a focused manner and build our relationships together in tranquil, scenic, and almost spiritual environment.

"We ensure that there is a fair amount of time for team building activities, socializing, good dining, and some fun activities in addition to the planning activities that generally need to take place in a meeting room. The retreat agenda is customized depending on the circumstances as it varies from situation to situation. However, for most ventures, the following process generally works quite well. Also, you can adopt this agenda to help you improve your score in the game of golf. Perhaps that's why golf has become the game of business. And as another bonus, this process even works unbelievably well for personal life planning as well!"

Ken paused a moment to allow Jake time to consider these ideas. Then he spoke up again. "A good starting point is to conduct a background review of your venture. Ensuring everyone knows about the company's evolution is a great starting point to bring everyone to a common understanding of the company. Just like it's great to know who designed a golf course and to develop a common understanding of the history of a club before you play gives you a greater appreciation for the course, it's also a good practice for team members to have a common knowledge about the history and evolution of your business," Ken explained.

"OK, that's pretty straight forward," Jake said. "What next?"

"Then, a good next step is to have your team conduct an environment overview," Ken explained. "This step examines the external factors that impact the game you're playing. In golf, it's the formation of the hole, examining fairway, hazards, trees, weather, slope and all of the other 'external' factors we discussed earlier today. For a business, it's all about stuff that may be political, economic, social, technological and more. Once again, it's best to get input on this from your entire team."

"I think I get it," said Jake. "It's like the team's collaborative view of the big picture and what external events may have an impact on the game we are playing."

"That's right," Ken confirmed. "Then, ideally, comes a review of market research, which has ideally been conducted and debriefed in advance of the retreat. In golf, it's like investing in a guidebook for a course that you have never played before. If you take the time to analyze the information ahead of the round, it'll tell you about the hole, what to expect, where to aim, what to avoid and where your misses need to be. Similarly, market research in business is a very wise use of investment resources that will allow your team to keep abreast of the market. At the most basic level, you need to get the team's input about the market needs from the various members of your team. At a higher level, it is an investment in intelligence about your customers that is best done by an independent professional who surveys your existing and potential customers to develop a comprehensive and honest understanding of their wants, needs, expectations, buyer behavior, future wants and your current position relative to your competitors.

"This research can also be done in focus groups, and it may also include additional research on industry data that identifies industry growth trends, alternative industry statistics and more. Market research is extremely valuable intelligence that will provide you with insights and knowledge to ensure you make the right decisions about where you should take your business. It helps you develop your strategy from the outside in. It ensures that you are relevant and adding value to your customers and the marketplace. This market research needs to be developed regularly and shared with the leaders of the different functional areas of your team as part of the strategic planning process."

"Yeah, yeah," Jake said dismissively. "We've all been hit on by these guys, usually at dinner time when the food goes on the table. Don't you think that doing market research is an expensive proposition?"

"Yes, but it is also a valuable investment, or perhaps, you could even consider it insurance against potential failure. Not doing it on a regular basis can cause you to miss a big opportunity, or perhaps even worse, result in missing a major change in the marketplace that could devastate your business. In one way it's like playing a new golf course after the second or third time. It's always easier, and you'll score better if you know what to expect. Also, on the downside, it can be like buying personal disability insurance. If you don't need to use it, you're happy because you're healthy, even though you had to pay for it. But if you throw out your back out on the golf course and can't work, you sure bet you are glad you bought it!"

"OK, OK, I can see the benefits of market research and understand about the pain!" Jake replied, faking a sore back. "What's next?"

"Next, comes a SWOT analysis. This is not some fancy electronic gizmo that evaluates your swing speed. It is a group activity done by your team, sometimes with the input of some board members and even outsiders. SWOT stands for Strengths, Weaknesses, Opportunities and Threats. Just like we spent some time examining your own golf game's strengths and weaknesses and the opportunities and threats out on the course, you need to get your business team to do this analysis for your company.

"When you do this, it's usually best to split your team leaders up into smaller groups where they will feel more comfortable communicating with one another. Then, have them brainstorm on each of these areas. Next, have them re-convene and share their thoughts with the team, who then validates and adds to their thinking," Ken outlined.

"That makes sense. Just like today's round, it'll give everyone a clear picture of what we're good at, what areas need improvement, where we could possibly focus our efforts, and where we definitely need to stay away from. Hey, I like this game. It's starting to sound a lot like golf!" Jake laughed.

"I thought you'd catch on pretty quick...just like earlier today," coached Ken.

"Then comes the goal line. The goal line is the target or bull's-eye for the team to shoot for somewhere in the future that they create a series of SMART goals for," Ken described.

"Whoa. Run that one by me again."

"Yes, the goal line is one of the most important parts of the strategic planning process. It provides a future target for the team to focus on. Just like targeting on your bull's-eye was a key to success in your golf game earlier today, the goal line is critical to success for your business team. During this process, the team establishes a time horizon for the future. Usually, it is two or three years out if the company situation is healthy. It can be a year or much less if the team is in a turnaround situation. Then, everyone on the team is encouraged to brainstorm and do some blue sky thinking to visualize their ideas about what they would love to achieve in the future. During the brainstorming part of the process, all ideas are encouraged and recorded, while no negative thoughts are allowed. Once everyone has run out of ideas / concepts, the team then goes through the brainstorming possibilities, decides what categories they belong in, and determines whether they are valid topics for discussion.

Then, it is time to do some critical evaluation and pare down the possibilities and determine specifically what the team intends to work towards. If possible, the targets are refined into SMART goals. SMART goals are specific, measurable, achievable, realistic and time limited ones. As you can imagine, this can be a very delicate discussion since these goals all overlap into one another's areas of responsibility. They are also the future measure by which the team is working towards and will be measured against. This work benefits significantly from a positive facilitator with a highly specialized skill set who has done this with all sorts of groups and can both encourage ideas, help resolve which ones are appropriate, and put some teeth into them so that they are realistic targets for the entire team shoot for. Then the team can clearly visualize or preview their collective picture of the future and the goals that form the basis of their bull's-eye target!"

"You know I can do that," said Jake excitedly. "I'm good at setting goals and making them happen."

"You think so?" Ken said knowingly. "That may be true for you personally, but what about in a group situation? What do you think happens if you, their dominant superior, is moderating this kind of discussion, and you challenge your team's ideas, especially if the person is a level or two below you in the organization hierarchy?

"Remember, you are a very powerful, dominant person, and I bet that your presence and energy tends to frighten others and shut some of your people down without you even realizing it occurs. When I was your age, I used to try to do this myself, but learned the hard way that my team planning sessions very quickly turned into a one-way communication where I was just laying out all of my ideas and thought that they were buying into my dream. Now that felt good because I like to be in control and tell people what to do. It was a boost for the big ego that is required from a leader, and I felt like a real General commanding the troops.

"However, the reality was that my team stopped listening, didn't buy in, tuned out or worse, started to even resent me for bossing them around. And you know what? This situation has changed significantly since I was your age. People are far less tolerant of this kind of "bossy" behavior. Over the last few decades, I have noticed that this kind of behavior is far less effective now than it was when I was your age...and it wasn't even effective then!"

"How about getting someone else on the team to do it then?" Jake suggested.

"Yeah, that's better, but they still have a vested interest in influencing the outcome to meet their own needs and will not be perceived as neutral. Your best choice, if you are budget constrained, is to have an outsider or a friend of the business do it. However, if at all possible and you can afford the investment, it is far better to have an experienced professional facilitate the process and then manage it an ongoing basis," Ken said.

"That makes sense." Jake mused. "But, what if I don't like or agree with what the team comes up with or leans towards?"

"Of course as the leader you always have the right to determine your final goal line target. Fortunately, having done this on numerous occasions, I have learned that the team comes up with ninety-five percent of what I would like them to target, and I only have to tweak their thinking to ensure it is on line with both my and our shareholders' interests. Let me explain. Over the years, I have experienced that this regular activity fosters what may be the most successful leadership style...that of the 'benevolent ruler'. Under this approach, the leader consults with the other members of the kingdom and whenever possible, goes with the team's consensual decision. However, if the ruler disagrees with the group thinking, or if there is a conflict, then the ruler will listen to various sides of the argument and then makes a ruling that the ruler deems to be in the best interest of the kingdom."

"Just like King Arthur...or like Arnold Palmer?" Jake smiled.

"Yeah, just like the King!" Ken laughed. "Now, here comes an extremely powerful technique that very few people on the planet know. As you learned earlier today during the round, the way to create a new program in the sub-conscious mind is to visualize or 'preview' the result that you would like to produce in your conscious mind and then use your senses to lock it in to the subconscious before allowing it to occur. The subconscious mind is the part of your brain that regulates automatic functions like your heart rate and breathing. Just like executing a golf swing, the subconscious mind works continuously in the background on automatic without you having to think about it.

"The underlying program that resides in your subconscious mind produces the result that has already been embedded into your mind. Fortunately, just like in our golf game, we have the ability to modify or re-write our program through introducing or embedding a new program through the conscious mind into the subconscious mind. We do this through consciously creating the preview of what we want to have as our outcome.

The subconscious mind is a more primitive part of the mind, and it processes in pictures or visuals rather than words. The big secret or technique to use in order to embed new programming into your subconscious mind is to imagine a multi-sensory, colorful image with all of your senses that the outcome you desire has already occurred while using positive emotions in order to lodge it as part of you new subconscious program, just like we did on the course. As you can appreciate, this is pretty deep stuff. In the team situation, we are working with a group of minds, and we need to have a powerful process to implant it into the subconscious mind of the entire group. This is where an expert trained in this field can help internalize such powerful new internal programming."

"Now that's interesting," Jake stated. "You mean that by internalizing a common shared vision in the group's subconscious mind it will significantly increase the likelihood of success?"

"Exactly," confirmed Ken. "Many people think in words, but many more think in pictures. About fifty percent of what we take in is visual, approximately thirty percent is auditory, and the rest comes in through the other senses. As part of our team visualization process, we have used a team drawing technique called the picture gallery before preparing our goal line. This is a group activity to have sub-groups of your team create a picture of the future on a flip chart of what their shared image of future success looks like and then share them with one another. Just like practicing on the range and locking in a good shot for you to recall for use on the course really works in golf. These visual images are very powerful and entertaining, with the team members having great fun reviewing their drawings. These positive emotions immediately cause the picture of the future to be lodged into the group's subconscious program.

"We build our goal line interactively with the use of a computer and project it onto a large screen for all to see and work from. In order to ensure all team members develop and intake information, it is best if there is a multi-media approach used. The team drafts its own work in real time, and it is all written up on the screen in the team's own words for everyone to see and work from. We craft the team goal line first by brainstorming, then categorizing, validating, prioritizing and sorting extremely quickly using some pretty cool outlining software.

"Psychologically, we are all continually reading and verbally reviewing our common goals for the future, and this multi-media approach and our own speaking voices reinforces the effect to ensure the goal line becomes a part of the entire team's subconscious program," Ken shared.

"Very interesting. Then what?" Ken asked.

"Then, after developing the goal line, which, as you can imagine, can take quite a bit of time and healthy debate to establish, we then apply another extremely powerful programming technique to embed our picture of the future in the team's subconscious. We have our team stand together and recite our goal line or a condensed version of it together with positive energy, action and emotion. Although we felt a bit funny doing this at first, the team usually gets right into it.

"Just as religious groups have used this technique with prayer to impact the faiths of their congregations for centuries, a business leader can use a similar approach to modify the behavior of his team. Most importantly, doing this together on a regular basis creates a powerful emotional bond, a team commitment to one another, and most importantly, it provides the conduit directly into the subconscious mind of each of the participants as well as the common mind of the team," Ken relayed.

"Wow!" Said Jake. "Is this stuff legal? Are we allowed to program people, and is it morally right to play with their subconscious mind?"

"Remember," Ken said, "all of the team members have the opportunity to contribute and validate each goal and for the common set of goals, so they all want to achieve the team's target. Secondly, I don't believe we can force people to do anything against their will using this type of team approach. Besides, we are doing positive work towards achieving a positive purpose and goals. We are empowering our people to achieve both their own individual purpose and our team's collective purpose. We truly ensure our team members are working towards achieving their potential, and this turns into exceptionally rewarding and profitable work."

"I guess so. Especially if I can use this knowledge to really improve my handicap," a relieved Jake said.

"Then, it's best to establish both critical success factors and the key performance indicators for the team to measure progress against. Both of these terms are pretty self-explanatory. The critical success factors are the activities that you absolutely need to do exceptionally well to achieve your goals. The key performance indicators are the measures that you establish to keep track and stay on target," explained Ken.

"So," Jake jumped in, "if your goal is to break ninety on a par seventy-two golf course or a score of eighteen over par, then a critical success factor could be to avoid making double or triple bogies, and a key performance indicator would be to average one shot better than one over par on each hole."

"Yeah, that's a pretty good analogy!" Ken said excitedly, filing the thought away for a future lesson. "Another example for a critical success factor for most players would be to invest more time practicing chipping and putting, as that's where more than 50% of most players' strokes are. An example of three key performance indicators in golf is to regularly track fairways hit in regulation, greens in regulation and putts per round."

"OK, that all makes sense to me. What's next?"

"Well, the next step is a confidential submission and identification of the current and perceived hurdles preventing the team from achieving its goals. Hurdles are like hazards on the golf course, but in the real world, we can't always see them as many of them are locked away in people's minds. It is vital to ensure everyone on the team has a trusted process and opportunity to confidentially submit their hurdles. These hurdles are major issues, concerns, obstacles, problems or challenges that are real or imagined that your team believes may be preventing the team from achieving its goal line.

"In order to maximize a team's performance the hurdles have to be drawn out from the team on a regular basis. As you can imagine, building a big long list of hurdles can be pretty depressing sometimes. You need to be upbeat and ensure the team with a big list of hurdles is pretty standard fare, and that they can be all be resolved or dealt with somehow.

"Yeah," Jake mused. "I can see for some people that revealing their challenges could be pretty threatening."

"Yes. However, in order to enrich the health, well being and future growth of any enterprise, a leader must have the courage to get his team to uncover any issues or concerns they may harbor before they turn into a cancer and cause greater harm to the venture. Fortunately, in my experience, there are very few hurdles that are not insurmountable, and addressing them demonstrates great leadership, honesty and integrity. These are the foundations that are absolutely necessary to building a dynamic, winning team."

"Hmm…so that's like a friend pointing out a swing flaw that'll cause tendonitis in your elbow. It may be tough to change in the short run, but it'll help improve your ability and your longevity to perform in the game."

"Hey, you're getting pretty good at this. Soon you'll be coaching others to go through this process yourself. As I mentioned previously, hurdles are kind of like hazards on the golf course. They are a big part of the game and even make the game interesting and enjoyable. After all, what fun would a golf game be without any hazards? Besides, a lot of the greatest businesses have been created as a result of solving a problem. Then, the hurdles lead to the next crucial step in the process."

"I can't wait." Jake said eagerly.

"Next comes the action plan. The action plan is a three-step process to build a high-level team to-do list. These action items can be major ongoing repeat activities or shorter-term projects and assignments. In order to produce an action plan, the first step is to have the team enter into a discussion and come with a resolution for all of the hurdles. That means determining the right action or series of actions that will allow the team to somehow eliminate, reduce or negate each and every hurdle. It is best to resolve the hurdles first, as many people can't or won't take any action unless the hurdles have been addressed. Once they have been dealt with, it is very liberating to the entire team and significantly encourages forward momentum," Ken shared.

"Just like today on the course, we either played around the hazards, over them or just did our best to ignore them when they didn't impact play. Once we were able to negotiate around them, it made the golf so round much easier. Can't we do the same thing with hurdles?" Jake questioned.

"Exactly," Ken confirmed. "That's the first step in the action plan process. Come up with a definitive action statement, usually a short sentence that begins with a verb like 'produce, make, establish, create, manage', build, grow, etc. Once we agree on the best course of action, we establish a target completion date or recurring dates for the task or activity."

"OK, that makes sense. Then what?" Jake asked.

"The next step in preparing an action plan," Ken offered, "is to go back to the goal line and review it so that your team identifies any other actions that need to be undertaken that haven't already been covered by tackling the hurdles. Interestingly, by resolving the hurdles, we have found that a significant number of goal line items have already been put into motion."

"I think I get it. Basically, we come up with a big to-do list that first resolves the hurdles, then we come up with any other to-do's that ensure we achieve the future goal line targets. Then what?"

"Now, having a neutral party facilitate this is one of the best parts for us leaders. Not only do we get to participate in the process, but also our guy gets the team members to volunteer and champion the tasks with other team members that need to participate in the task. If I don't agree, then I speak up and assign other people, but amazingly, the right people generally volunteer themselves. This is very powerful as it widens the circle of commitment not just to me, their leader, but also to their entire team. As a result, their level of commitment is substantially higher as they have provided both a verbal and written 'contract' to their peers as well as to me. We work through the entire list to ensure that each goal line target has an action plan list of high level activities with target completion dates and a champion accountable for getting it done!"

"Wow. So you end up with your team volunteering to make commitments to action and a time line for completion! And you don't have to tell them what, when or how to do it! Sound's great. Sign me up!" Jake cheered.

"Yeah!" Ken confirmed. "The best part about it, of course, is that the team is highly committed, engaged, positive, and ready to take the lead to achieve our team's vision and goals. It's really exciting to see them get inspired and engaged on an ongoing basis. All I do is then monitor the progress on their activities and allocate resources as required."

"Now that's really exciting." Jake relayed. "I've always wanted my team to be really motivated and inspired towards achieving our goals!"

"Here's another significant key to ensuring execution," Ken advised. "Not only is doing this type of activity important, but also ensuring you do it on an ongoing basis is what truly produces results. Just like going through a consistent planning process in your golf game prior to each round, hole and shot is critical to ensuring your best results, it is critical in your business to ensure that you and your team have a disciplined, ongoing, consistent process in place that you follow on an ongoing basis. It's just like practicing on the range and on the putting green. Doing it once is helpful, but regular, disciplined practice and repetition that leads to sound execution on an ongoing basis is what truly produces exceptional results."

"Yeah, that makes sense. I know if I could take the time to practice my golf game regularly that I could easily be a single digit handicap," confirmed Jake.

"Exactly," replied Ken. "We get together on an ongoing basis to ensure that we not only set, but that we achieve our goals. An ongoing regular disciplined process reduces my having to oversee the team and really drives results. When the team knows that we have this process in place and we have quarterly update meetings with our team's coach, it's like having a deadline, and we all know that the majority of work gets done when there is a deadline in place."

"Yeah," confirmed Jake, "Just like the pros getting their game in shape for the Major's. It seems that's when they really focus on their game and get themselves ready to play at their peak!"

"Best of all," Ken mentioned, "Our guy has really performed and has stood by his work. On a multi-year program, we structured his compensation so that a substantial portion of his fee is tied to our improving our business team's results. It leads to a real partnership relationship with all of us.

"He and his firm also do work with some of the country's leading venture capitalists, private equity players and board members who had the foresight to see the value in providing these services in conjunction with their investment in companies. These savvy players recognize that having this activity done regularly with their companies reduces their own personal work load, gives them additional insight into their investments, and most importantly, helps them drive growth and real results much faster than the ventures would without such a support to leadership process in place. The operating teams really enjoy the activity and are the primary beneficiaries of the work. Ensuring that an ongoing, disciplined strategic planning process is in place ensures that the companies and their teams are focused on achieving growth, overcoming hurdles and achieving both their human and business potential. It's truly a win / win situation."

"You know," Ken continued, "various public companies that have done this type of work tend to increase the share price within a pretty short period of time. Our guy's firm even structure compensation with public companies based on them achieving significant share value increases, as well!"

"I like that approach," Jake agreed. "We currently have equity options for senior management and profit sharing for other team members. We are even looking at putting employee ownership programs in place. I agree that having everyone's interests aligned leads to higher likelihood of achieving a successful outcome."

"Most importantly, though," Ken mentioned, "our guy has taken the time to get to know me and help me realize my own personal and business goals. Heck, he even helps me on the golf course! He has also been of great value to our company and the clean technology industries and practices that our planet and global economy desperately needs to thrive. We meet regularly every quarter to discuss and update both my personal career activities and our team purpose, strategy and execution plans. In addition, we get out for a round or two of golf a year with one or two of his other leadership clients so that we can spend some social time together. Of course, this also helps improve our golf game!"

"Well," said Jake, "You know my situation. Do you really think that that developing and maintaining an ongoing strategic game plan will help me build teamwork, grow our business, help me achieve my business goals, and maybe even improve my golf game? That's a pretty tall order!"

"Well, as you have heard, it has worked for me," said Ken. "If you like, here's my guy's name, number and his website."

"Thanks, Ken. That sounds really great," Jake replied. "I'll set up a get together see if it will work for me and my team. Your advice on my game has already proven to be better than par!"

The two gentlemen then went on to finish a thoroughly enjoyable lunch together. They then said their goodbyes to one another until the next golf season.

# CHAPTER 6
## THE SPRING AHEAD

# CHAPTER 6

It was a beautiful, warm spring afternoon, one of the first of the new golf season. Ken was warming up striping some balls out onto the range and looking forward to playing a round with some of his long-term golf and business buddies. Suddenly, Jake pulled up to the range and saw Ken. He headed over with a great big grin on his face.

"Hey, Ken, how the heck are you? Looks like the winter was good to you!" Jake had a laugh in his voice. "You're looking great. I bet you're doing well!" he exclaimed.

"Why, thank you," said Ken, glad to see that Jake was looking positive and energized. "I am well. How are you doing?"

"I'm doing great, too. I heard you were here, and I've been all over the course looking for you so that I can thank you in person," Jake said emphatically.

"Thank me? For what?" Asked Ken.

"I wanted to thank you for your late fall golf coaching last year. I applied your strategy on a golf holiday and played my best rounds ever!"

"That's great!" said Ken sincerely.

"Not only that, but I also wanted to thank you for referring me to your team's strategic coach. After our round together last fall, I connected with him and set up a meeting. I liked him and his style. We spent some time together discussing our company, my team, our industry, my personal goals and passions. He designed a customized program that fit my needs and budget. It helped me and the leaders of my team build and execute our own team strategic plan!

"We conducted some market research, did some team psychological assessments and then held a strategic planning retreat with the team. It was a highly challenging and invigorating activity for everyone on the team. We learned some great insights about our customers and competition. We brainstormed a great team purpose and put in place a solid game plan. It was really tough work; as I had to really open up with my team in order to build a higher level of trust with them.

"As you can imagine, we had to tackle some major hurdles and are all now really focused on getting the work done. As a result of building our team game plan, conducting our talent assessments and alignment around personal goals, we found that we needed to re-arrange the positions of a couple of our team members. It was the right thing for the team, but I felt bad since I had to let go of a couple long-term team members, as they no longer fit in with the ideal team profile. Fortunately, we were able to help one find a great position with one of our suppliers and helped another transition into a different industry. You know, I have heard that both of them are happier now, as they have found be a better fit with their personal purposes, goals and abilities.

"Most importantly, ever since our retreat, our newly aligned team has been engaged, energized, and working unbelievably well together. We have recruited a couple of new team members whose profile and behavior have really complemented our mix. It has given all of us a great common view for the future that we all believe in and are all driving towards. It's like we've taken a huge leap forward and we are really springing ahead!

"Already, our profitability is starting to improve, our sales are trending upwards, our technology development path is accelerating and our team is humming. We have a lot of work ahead of us, but I no longer have to focus all my energy on directing the team so closely. They seem to have taken it upon themselves to make the majority of the right decisions. I find that I'm not nagging them to show initiative, and they have really risen to a higher level of performance. They all seem to be doing this while working the same or even fewer hours, which is great as they have the time to recharge with friends and families.

"It's all working out so well that I have committed to an ongoing team strategic planning program to drive results with my team for the next three years of future growth! Best of all, I now have significantly more time to focus my energy on the purpose, strategy and execution levels for my team, my company and myself. I really believe that I am becoming a much better leader and a better man. With the improvement at our business level, it has even helped improved my personal life with family and friends. Hey, I've even got some time to work on my golf game!" Jake exclaimed.

"Hey," Said Ken, "that's great news. I'm so glad that you are looking so positive and that everything is working out so well for you and your team. Hey, how about a replay of our match in a couple of weeks? Maybe this time you might take me to the eighteenth hole!" Ken jokingly teased.

"Love to," Jake responded. "Do you think you're ready to take me on?"

"I'm sure looking forward to it!" Ken challenged with a smile.

As he headed off to play his round Jake laughed. "Enjoy the game!"

# CHAPTER 7
## EAGLES AND TEAMS

# CHAPTER 7

Eagles are the exceptional business and social leaders who are the visionary drivers that possess great insight, vision and talent. Eagles reside at the top of the economic food chain and are the highly gifted members of our society who have the ability to drive innovation, wealth creation and prosperity for all.

Eagles have tremendous strength, abilities and potential. Although many eagles sometimes begin their careers as predators, the greatest eagles evolve to enable others to fly in formation and produce great wealth and prosperity for themselves, for others, for humanity and for the continuation of life on our planet.

Independent research studies have validated that these leaders and teams who engage in developing and maintaining a sound strategic plan on a regular basis significantly increase their business performance, while also increasing employee satisfaction

Over the years I have had been extremely fortunate to have had many teachers and mentors in the games of golf, business and life. My greatest learnings have come from working directly with many great eagles of the different games. Hopefully, I have been able to communicate and share some of their insights to help you realize your potential in your game.

Sincerely,

## Max Carbone

**416-721-6359**

**max@teamworksweb.com**

**www.teamworksweb.com**

# NOTES

# NOTES

# OTHER BOOKS FROM LIFESUCCESS PUBLISHING

### SYSTEM OF SUCCESS

10 Principles of
Self Empowerment
to Enhance
Personal Performance

**Stephen
and Karen Byrne**

ISBN 978-1-59930-085-6

### BODY AWAKENING

Balance your Body,
Mind & Spirit with
PILATES and an
Active Lifestyle

**Karin Hagberg**

ISBN 978-1-59930-190-7

### THE VISIONARY LEADER

How to Inspire
Success from
the Top Down

**Susan Bagyura**

ISBN 978-1-59930-094-8

### FULL BODY ORGASM

Your Energy to
Love, Health,
Wealth, and
Happiness

**Oscar Naval**

ISBN 978-1-59930-200-3

### YOUR FACE YOUR CHOICE

Break the aging cycle.
The secret to a
refreshed and refined
YOU in 90 days - the
natural way.

**Wentzel &
Cynthia Coetzer**

ISBN 978-1-59930-125-9

### THE MAGNETIC CEO

A Handbook for
Attracting and
Retaining the
Brightest and the Best

**Dr. Dalia
R.E. Lavon**

ISBN 978-1-59930-079-5

### RE-CREATE THE SENIOR'S SOUL

Helping you achieve
a Healthy Lifestyle

**Anita Selby**

ISBN 978-1-59930-179-2

### UNLOCK YOUR FUTURE

The Key to a
Fullfiling Life

**Jan Peter
Aursnes**

ISBN 978-1-59930-217-1

# OTHER BOOKS FROM LIFESUCCESS PUBLISHING

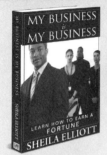

## MY BUSINESS IS MY BUSINESS

Learn How to Earn a Fortune

**Shelia Elliott**

ISBN 978-1-59930-149-5

## WE THE NEW ME

Unleash the Creative Power of Your Mind

**Debbii McKoy**

ISBN 978-159930104-4

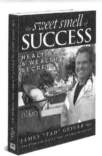

## THE SWEET SMELL OF SUCCESS

Health & Wealth Secrets

**James "Tad" Geiger M.D.**

ISBN 978-1-59930-088-7

## SEX

Do You Want More?

**Linda Wilde**

ISBN 978-1-59930-160-0

## GET THE RENOVATION YOU REALLY WANT!

Renovating your home should be a wonderful experience...

**John Salton**

ISBN 978-1-59930-169-3

## THE SUCCESS TOOLBOX

For Entrepreneurs

**Janis Vos**

ISBN 978-1-59930-005-4

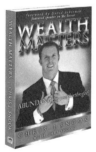

## WEALTH MATTERS

Abundance is Your Birthright

**Chris J. Snook with Chet Snook**

ISBN 978-1-59930-096-2

## THE GIRLZ GUIDE TO BUILDING WEALTH

...and men like it too

**Maya Galletta, Aaron Cohen, Polly McCormick, Mike McCormick**

ISBN 978-1-59930-048-1

# OTHER BOOKS FROM LIFESUCCESS PUBLISHING

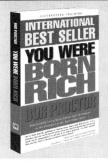

## YOU WERE BORN RICH

**Bob Proctor**

ISBN 978-0-9656264-1-5

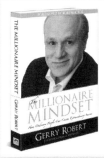

## THE MILLIONAIRE MINDSET

How Ordinary People Can Create Extraordinary Income

**Gerry Robert**

ISBN 978-1-59930-030-6

## REKINDLE THE MAGIC IN YOUR RELATIONSHIP

Making Love Work

**Anita Jackson**

ISBN 978-1-59930-041-2

## FINDING THE BLOOM OF THE CACTUS GENERATION

Improving the Quality of Life for Seniors

**Maggie Walters**

ISBN 978-1-59930-011-5

## THE BEVERLY HILLS SHAPE

The Truth About Plastic Surgery

**Dr. Stuart Linder**

ISBN 978-1-59930-049-8

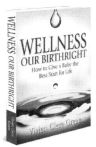

## WELLNESS OUR BIRTHRIGHT

How to give a baby the Best Start in Life

**Vivien Clere Green**

ISBN 978-1-59930-020-7

## LIGHTEN YOUR LOAD

**Peter Field**

ISBN 978-1-59930-000-9

## CHANGE & HOW TO SURVIVE IN THE NEW ECONOMY

7 Steps to Finding Freedom & Escaping the Rat Race

**Barrie Day**

ISBN 978-1-59930-015-3

# OTHER BOOKS FROM LIFESUCCESS PUBLISHING

## STOP SINGING THE BLUES

10 Powerful Strategies For Hitting The High Notes In Your Life

**Dr. Cynthia Barnett**

ISBN 978-1-59930-022-1

## DON'T BE A VICTIM! PROTECT YOURSELF

Everything Seniors Need To Know To Avoid Being Taken Financially

**Jean Ann Dorrell**

ISBN 978-1-59930-024-5

## A "HAND UP," NOT A "HAND OUT"

The Best Ways to Help Others HelpThemselves

**David Butler**

ISBN 978-1-59930-071-9

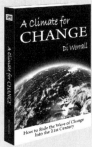

## A CLIMATE FOR CHANGE

How to ride the Wave of Change into the 21st Century

**Di Worrall**

ISBN 978-1-59930-123-5

## I BELIEVE IN ME

7 Ways for Woman to Step Ahead in Confidence

**Lisa Gorman**

ISBN 978-1-59930-069-6

## THE COLOR OF SUCCESS

Why Color Matters in your Life, your Love, your Lexus

**Mary Ellen Lapp**

ISBN 978-1-59930-078-8

## IF NOT NOW, WHEN?

What's Your Dream?

**Cindy Nielsen**

ISBN 978-1-59930-073-3

## THE SKILLS TO PAY THE BILLS... AND THEN SOME!

How to inspire everyone in your organisation into high performance!

**Buki Mosaku**

ISBN 978-1-59930-058-0